STRANGE BUT TRUE

Aliens

STRANGE BUT TRUE

Aliens

DAMON WILSON

PARRAGON

This edition published and distributed by
Parragon
Unit 13–17, Avonbridge Trading Estate
Atlantic Road
Avonmouth
Bristol, BS11 9QD

This edition produced by Magpie Books, an imprint
of Robinson Publishing Ltd. in 1997

British Library Cataloguing-in-Publication Data
A catalogue record for this book is available
from the British Library

ISBN 0–75252–134–9

Printed and bound in the E.C.

Contents

Introduction

Apemen – almost, but not quite human – are reported regularly in the deep forests of North America and the bleak mountain ranges of Tibet and China. Fairies, having escaped straight from children's books, are seen playing in fields and gardens – shaking sane, reputable witnesses with the knowledge that what they are seeing *cannot possibly exist*. A demonic vampire attacks thousands of farm animals in Central America, but cannot be caught. Weird, discarnate entities haunt and terrify climbers in the Scottish Cairngorm Mountains and a huge half-man, half-moth creature stalks the woods of West Virginia. These creatures, as much as any visitor in a UFO, can be said to be completely alien to mankind.

The word *alien* is commonly and widely used in everyday language. We utilize it to refer to things as diverse as plants foreign to an area of land, concepts we are unable to comprehend or more imaginatively, beings from another planet. The last of these – extraterrestrial visitors – will be a major focus of this book, but other aspects of "alien life" will also be considered, so a definition of the term, as it will be used here, is necessary.

The simplest common definition of an alien is something that is intelligent but not human. This is obviously too broad a description since it can arguably include dolphins, elephants, orang-utans and a dozen other "known" species. For a creature to be called an alien, it must also be vested with a certain element of the unknown.

In this book we will look at some of the strange beings that seem to haunt the fringes of our rationalistic, scientifically-structured world, but which we cannot automatically dismiss as fantasies because of a flow of new, well-authenticated sightings. The possibility that such creatures may be as native to the Earth as human beings should also remind us that, to them, it is *we* who are the aliens.

Almost Human – the Bigfoot, the Yeti and the Alma

Are human beings the only intelligent species of upright creature on the planet? Many would say that it is a self-evident fact. We humans may show respect for evolutionary relatives like chimpanzees, gorillas and orang-utans, but we never refer to them as "people". Even our species name, Homo sapiens, self-defines us as the thinking animal. Our Cro-Magnon ancestors earned the sole right to this title thirty thousand years ago, when they seem to have exterminated our closest rivals (and relatives) the Neanderthals. Since that time mankind has been the sole, lonely ruler of our planet.

Yet down through the millennia, tales of strange, hairy half-men have surfaced in almost every culture. Even in our age of helicopters, spy-satellites and disappearing natural habitats, such reports are far from rare. Are these ancient ghosts, a racial memory of our lost kin, or do demi-humans still survive in secluded corners of the modern world?

Big Foot

Like the gun-fight at the OK Corral, the siege of Ape Canyon has become part of American folklore.

The tale begins in 1924, when a group of miners were

working in the Mount St Helen's range in Washington State, seventy-five miles north of Portland, Oregon. One day they saw a big ape-like creature peering out from behind a tree. One of the miners fired at it and thought the bullet hit its head. The creature ran off into the forest. Then another miner, Fred Beck – who was to tell the story thirty-four years later – met another of the "apes" at the canyon rim and shot it in the back three times. It toppled over into the canyon; but when the miners went to look there was no body.

That night the miners found themselves under siege. From dusk until dawn the next day the creatures pounded on the doors, walls and the roof, and rocks were hurled. The miners braced the heavy door from inside and fired shots through the walls and roof. But the creatures were obviously angry and determined and the assault ceased only at sunrise. That day the miners decided to abandon the site.

Beck's description of the "Bigfoot" is of a creature about eight feet tall and very muscular. It looked not unlike a gorilla, but if it could use rocks as a weapon of assault, then it was clearly humanoid.

Fred Beck's account of the siege, together with other sightings on the west coast, made Bigfoot something of a national celebrity in the late 1950s. But stories about the creature had been in circulation for centuries. The Salish Indians of British Columbia called the creature "Sasquatch", meaning "wild man of the woods". In northern California the Huppa tribe call them "Oh-mah-ah"; in the Cascades they are known as "Seeahtiks".

The notion of colonies of monsters living quietly in the modern US and Canada admittedly sounds absurd; but this is partly because few people grasp the sheer size of the North American coniferous forests – thousands of square miles of totally uninhabited woodland, some still unexplored, where it would be possible to hide a herd of dinosaurs.

The first recorded story of a Sasquatch footprint dates back to 1811. The well-known explorer and trader, David Thompson, was crossing the Rockies towards the mouth of the Columbia river when, at the site of modern Jasper, Alberta, he and his companion came upon a footprint fourteen inches by eight inches, with four toes and claw marks. Thompson thought it was probably a grizzly bear, but his companion insisted that it couldn't have been because bears have five toes. In any case, few bears leave behind fourteen-inch footprints.

The *Daily Colonist* of Victoria, British Columbia, for Friday July 4 1884, published an account of the capture of a Bigfoot. Jacko (as his captors called him), seems to have been a fairly small specimen, only four feet, seven inches high, and weighing 127 pounds. He was spotted from a train which was winding its way along the Fraser river from Lytton to Yale, in the shadow of the Cascade mountains, and apparently captured without too much difficulty. He was described as having long black, coarse hair and short glossy hairs all over his body. The forearms were much longer than a man's, and were powerful enough to be able to tear a branch in two. Regrettably, Jacko's subsequent fate is unknown, although the naturalist John Napier reports that he may have been exhibited in Barnum and Bailey's Circus.

In 1910 Bigfoot was blamed for a gruesome event that took place in the Nahanni Valley, near Great Slave Lake in the Northwest Territories. Two brothers named MacLeod were found headless in the Valley, which subsequently became known as Headless Valley. It seems far more likely that the prospectors were murdered by Indians or desperados; nevertheless, Bigfoot was blamed, and the legend acquired a touch of horror.

In 1910 the *Seattle Times* contained a report about "mountain devils" who attacked the shack of a prospector at Mount St Lawrence, near Kelso. The attackers were described as half-human and half-monster, and between seven and eight feet tall. To the Clallam and Quinault Indians the creatures are known as "Seeahtiks". Their legends declare that man was created from animals, and that "Seeahtiks" were left in a half-finished state.

One of the most remarkable Bigfoot stories dates from 1924, although it was not written down until 1957 when it was uncovered by John Green, author of *On the Track of the Sasquatch*. Albert Ostman, a logger and construction worker, was looking for gold at the head of the Toba Inlet in British Columbia, and was unalarmed when an Indian boatman told him tales of "big people" living in the mountains. After a week's hiking he settled down in a campsite opposite Vancouver Island. But when he woke up in the morning he found that his supplies had been disturbed. He decided to stay awake that night, so when he climbed into his sleeping-bag he removed only his boots; he also took his rifle into the sleeping-bag with him. Hours later, he reported, "I was awakened by something picking me up. I was asleep and at first I did not remember where I was. As I began to get my wits together, I remembered I was on this prospecting trip, and in my sleeping-bag."

Hours later, his captor dumped him down on the ground, and he was able to crawl out of the sleeping-bag. He found himself in the presence of a family of four

Sasquatches – a father eight feet tall, a mother and teenage son and immature daughter. Ostman described them in considerable detail – the woman was over seven feet tall, between forty and seventy years of age, and weighed between 500 and 600 pounds. They apparently made no attempt to hurt him, but seemed determined not to let him go. Possibly they regarded him as a future husband for the girl, who was small and flat-chested. He spent six days in their company until, choosing his moment, he fired off his rifle. While his captors dived for cover, Ostman escaped. Asked by John Green why he had kept silent for so long, Ostman explained that he thought nobody would believe him.

In 1928 an Indian of the Nootka tribe called Muchalat Harry arrived at Nootka, on Vancouver Island, clad only in torn underwear, and still badly shaken. He explained that he had been making his way to the Conuma river to do some hunting and fishing when, like Ostman, he was picked up – complete with sleeping-bag – and carried several miles by a Bigfoot. At daybreak he found himself in the midst of a group of about twenty of the creatures, and was at first convinced they intended to eat him. When one of them tugged at his underwear it was obviously astonished that it was loose – assuming it to be his skin. He sat motionless for hours, and by afternoon they had lost interest and went off looking for food. Harry took the opportunity to escape, and ran a dozen or so miles to where he had hidden his canoe, then paddled another forty-five miles back to Vancouver Island, where he told this story to Father Anthony Terhaar, of the Benedictine Mission. Terhaar says that Harry was in such a state of nervous collapse that he needed to be nursed carefully back to health, and that

7

his hair became white. The experience shook him so much that he never again left the village.

In 1967 a logger called Glenn Thomas from Estacada, Oregon, was walking down a path at Tarzan Springs near the Round Mountain when he saw three big hairy figures pulling rocks out of the ground, then digging down six or seven feet. The male figure took out a nest of rodents and ate them. Investigators looking into his story found thirty or forty holes, from which rocks weighing as much as two hundredweight had been shifted. Chucks and marmots often hibernate under such rocks, and there were many of these animals in the area.

By that time one of the most convincing pieces of evidence for the existence of Bigfoot had emerged. In October 1967 two young men called Roger Patterson and Bob Gimlin were in Bluff Creek in Del Norte county, northern California, when they were thrown from their horses as they rounded the bend in the Creek. About a hundred feet ahead, on the other side of the Creek bed, there was a huge, hairy creature that walked like a man. Roger Patterson grabbed his ciné-camera, and started filming. The creature – which they had by now decided was a female – stopped dead, then looked around at them. "She wasn't scared a bit. The fact is, I don't think she was scared of *me*, and the only thing I can think of is that the clicking of my camera was new to her." As Patterson tried to follow her the creature suddenly began to run, and after three and a half miles they lost her tracks on pine needles.

The film – which has become famous – shows a creature about seven feet high, weighing around 350 to 450 pounds, with reddish-brown hair and prominent furry breasts and buttocks. As it strides past it turns its head and looks straight into the camera, revealing a fur-covered face. The top of the head is conical in shape. Both mountain gorillas and Bigfoot's cousin the Yeti or Abominable Snowman (of which more in a moment) display this feature. According to zoologists, its purpose is to give more anchorage to the jaw muscles to aid in breaking tough plants.

Inevitably, there were many scientists who dismissed the film as a hoax, claiming that the creature was a man dressed in a monkey suit. But in his book *More "Things"* the zoologist Ivan Sanderson quotes three scientists, Dr Osman Hill, Dr John Napier and Dr Joseph Raight, all of whom seem to agree that there is nothing in the film that leads them, on scientific grounds, to suspect a hoax. Casts taken of the footprints in the mud of the Creek indicate a creature roughly seven feet high.

The sheer size of the Bigfoot is a major cause of the public's skepticism. It is hard to believe that seven foot, 450 pound monsters live, almost undetected, in high-tech North America. If they were real, surely we would have captured a Sasquatch by now? Of course, when we say that the Bigfoot has escaped proper scrutiny, we really mean study by western science. It is worth remembering that today fewer people frequent the deep forests of North America than did in the days before Columbus. The nomad Native Americans, before the cultural impact of the white settlers, seem to have accepted the Sasquatch as a natural, if rare, part of the woodland environment. Is it possible that the Indian's pragmatic reaction was due to a more regular contact with the creature? As the playwright Tom Stoppard once observed, a man who sees one unicorn in his life will think it an amazing beast – if, on the other hand, he sees thousands, he will think them commonplace.

Photo of a Bigfoot taken in 1973 in Washington, USA

It is also worth bearing in mind that the gorilla, Africa's largest known ape, was little more than a myth to European science up until the mid-nineteenth century. Gorillas remained "undiscovered" because they lived in uninhabited forests, not because they were determined to hide from people. Reports seem to show that the Sasquatch not only live in distant woodlands, but that they also try to avoid at all cost being seen by humans.

This leads us to speculate about the intelligence of the Bigfoot. Do they avoid human contact out of natural shyness, or do mother Sasquatches warn their children to avoid the "dangerous smooth-skinned dwarfs?" The question is not as flippant as it sounds. Albert Ostman's account of a well-ordered Bigfoot family, the tale of the coordinated attack on the cabin at Ape Canyon and hundreds of reported sightings point to a more than ape-like intelligence. (Many sightings come from drivers who glance into their rear-view mirror to see the creature rise up from the side of the road and hurriedly cross after the vehicle has passed: behavior more akin to a human fugitive than an animal.)

In fact, several Bigfoot witnesses actually claim to have heard the creatures speak. In the summer of 1956, sixteen-year-old Cliff Crook and three friends were camping in the woods of Washington State. Sitting around the fire one night, they wondered at what was causing their dog to bark and rush to a nearby area of swamp. Hidden in the semi-darkness, something huge picked up the dog and hurled it back towards the campsite. The boys bravely held their ground and threw flaming sticks from the campfire at the intruder. Then "we heard a horrendous sound," Crook told a reporter for the *Seattle News Tribune*. "Not a language we knew. 'Ee-gor-lar-gor.' Deep and heavy." A giant hairy figure then strode into the circle of firelight and the boys ran for their lives. Not surprisingly, Cliff Crook has been fascinated by the Bigfoot ever since and has run a Sasquatch report monitoring group called "Bigfoot Central" for the last fifteen years. In an interview in the *Fortean Times* (December 1996), he claimed the group receives about twenty telephone calls a week, "perhaps three reporting a sighting." At around 150 possible sightings a year, that makes Bigfoot more common than many endangered species.

The Yeti

The Asian version of Bigfoot is the Yeti, better known as the Abominable Snowman. When Eric Shipton, the Everest explorer, was crossing the Menlung Glacier on Everest in 1951 he observed a line of huge footprints; Shipton photographed one of them, with an ice axe beside it to provide scale. It was eighteen inches long and thirteen inches wide, and its shape was curious – three small toes and a huge big toe that seemed to be almost circular. The footsteps were those of a two-legged creature, not a wolf or a bear. The only animal with a vaguely similar foot is an orang-utan. But they have a far longer big toe.

Ever since European travellers began to explore Tibet they had reported legends of a huge ape-like creature called the Metoh-kangmi, which translates roughly as the filthy or abominable snowman. The stories cover a huge area, from the Caucasus to the Himalayas, from the

Pamirs, through Mongolia, to the far eastern tip of Russia. In central Asia they are called Mehteh, or Yetis, while tribes of eastern Asia refer to them as Almas. The earliest reference to them in the West seems to be a report in 1832 by B. H. Hodgson, the British Resident at the Court of Nepal, who mentioned that his native hunters were frightened by a "wild man" covered in long dark hair. More than half a century later, in 1889, Major L. A. Waddell was exploring the Himalayas when he came across huge footprints in the snow at 17,000 feet; his bearers told him that these were the tracks of a Yeti. And the Yeti, according to the bearers, was a ferocious creature which was quite likely to attack human beings and carry them off for food. The best way to escape it was to run downhill, for the Yeti had such long hair that it would fall over its eyes and blind it.

In 1921 an expedition led by Colonel Howard Bury, making a first attempt on the north face of Everest, saw in the distance a number of large dark creatures moving against the snow of the Lhapta-la Pass; the Tibetan porters said these were Yetis. And in 1925, N. A. Tombazi, a Fellow of the Royal Geographical Society, almost managed to get a photograph of a naked, upright creature on the Zemu Glacier; but it had vanished by the time he sighted the camera. And so the legends and the sightings continued to leak back to civilization, always with that slight element of doubt which made it possible for scientists to dismiss them as lies or mistakes. Shipton's photograph of 1951 caused such a sensation because it was taken by a member of a scientific expedition who could have no possible motive for stretching the facts. Besides, the photograph spoke for him.

The Australian version of Bigfoot is the *Yowie*. Seen in various wooded parts of the country, this hulking creature bears a strong resemblance to both the Siberian Alma and the North American Sasquatch. For example, in 1978, a National Parks and Wildlife ranger claimed to have seen the creature in Queensland's Lamington National Park. He described it as a "big, black, hairy man-thing." It was around eight feet tall, was very muscular and had piercing yellow eyes. The pair stood staring at each other for about ten minutes, then the *Yowie* released a foul odor and bounded into the woods. This was only one of a wave of similar sightings in the park during that year.

It might be tempting to think of the *Yowie* as an Australian copy of an American media fad, but the creature has a long history. Aboriginal folktales recount battles between the *Yowies* and the first human settlers of Australia. Paul Cropper, a researcher who has extensively studied *Yowie* reports suggested in an interview (in the *Fortean Times*, no. 76), that the creatures may have been the original inhabitants of the continent. Whether they survive as projections of ancestral memories or actually in the flesh, however, remains a bone of contention among cryptozoologists.

At least, so one might assume. The Natural History Department of the British Museum did not agree, and one of its leading authorities, Dr T. C. S. Morrison-Scott, was soon committing himself to the view that the footprint was made by a creature called the Himalayan langur. His assessment was based on a description of the

Yeti by Sherpa Tensing, who said it was about five feet high, walked upright, had a conical skull and reddish-brown fur. This, said Dr Morrison-Scott, sounded quite like a langur. The objection to this was that the langur, like most apes, walks on all fours most of the time; besides, its feet have five very long toes, quite unlike the four rounded toes of the photograph. Morrison-Scott's theory was greeted with hoots of disdain, as it undoubtedly deserved to be. But that brought the identification of the strange creature no closer.

A more imaginative view was taken by the Dutch zoologist Bernard Huevelmans in a series of articles published in Paris in 1952. He pointed out that in 1934, Dr Ralph von Koenigwald had discovered some ancient teeth in the shop of a Chinese apothecary in Hong Kong – the Chinese regard powdered teeth as a medicine. One of these was a human-type molar which was twice as large as the molar of an adult gorilla, suggesting that its owner had stood about twelve feet tall. Evidence suggested that this giant – he became known as Gigantopithecus – lived around half a million years ago. Huevelmans suggested that Shipton's footprints were made by a huge biped related to Gigantopithecus. But few scientists considered his theory seriously.

In 1954 the *Daily Mail* sent out an expedition to try to capture (or at least photograph) a Yeti. It spent fifteen weeks plodding through the Himalayan snows without so much as a glimpse of the filthy snowman. But the expedition gathered one exciting piece of information. Several monasteries, they learned, possessed "Yeti scalps", which were revered as holy relics. Several of these scalps were tracked down, and proved to be fascinating. They were all long and conical, rather like a bishop's mitre, and covered with hair, including a "crest" in the middle, made of erect hair. One of these scalps proved to be a fake, sewn together from fragments of animal skin. But others were undoubtedly made of one piece of skin. Hairs from them were sent to experts for analysis, and the experts declared that they came from no known animal. It looked as if the existence of the Yeti had finally been proved. Alas, it was not to be.

Sir Edmund Hillary was allowed to borrow one of the scalps – he was held in very high regard in Tibet – and Bernard Huevelmans had the opportunity to examine it. It reminded him of a creature called the southern serow, a kind of goat, which he had seen in a zoo before the war. And serows exist in Nepal, "Abominable Snowman" country. Huevelmans tracked down a serow in the Royal Institute in Brussels. And comparison with the Yeti scalp revealed that it came from the same animal. The skin had been stretched and moulded with steam. It was not, of course, a deliberate fake. It was made to be worn in certain religious rituals in Tibet; over the years its origin had been forgotten, and it had been designated a Yeti scalp.

All this was enough to convince the sceptics that the Yeti was merely a legend. But that conclusion was premature. Europeans who went out searching for the snowman might or might not catch a glimpse of some dark creature moving against the snow. But their tracks were observed, and photographed, in abundance. A Frenchman, the Abbé Bordet, followed three separate lots of tracks in 1955. Squadron Leader Lester Davies filmed huge footprints in the same year. Climber Don Whillans saw an ape-like creature on Annapurna in June 1970, and Lord Hunt photographed more Yeti tracks in 1978.

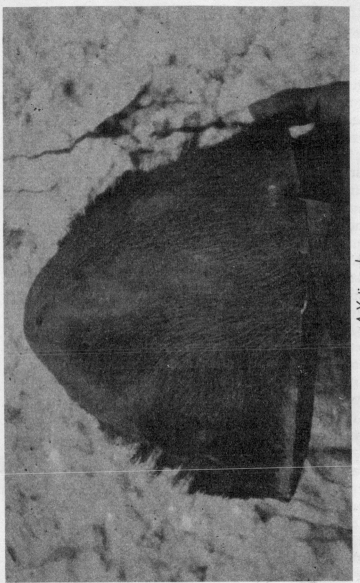

A Yeti scalp

Alma

In Russia more solid evidence began to emerge. In 1958 Lt Col Vargen Karapetyan saw an article on the Yeti – or, as it is known in Russia, Alma – in a Moscow newspaper, and sought out the leading Soviet expert, Professor Boris Porshnev, to tell him his own story. In December 1941 his unit had been fighting the Germans in the Caucasus near Buinakst, and he was approached by a unit of partisans and asked to go and look at a man they had taken prisoner. The partisans explained that Karapetyan would have to go along to a barn to look at the "man", because as soon as he was taken into a heated room, he stank and dripped sweat; besides, he was covered in lice. The "man" proved to be more like an ape: naked, filthy and unkempt, he looked dull and vacant, and often blinked. He made no attempt to defend himself when Karapetyan pulled out hairs from his body, but his eyes looked as if he was begging for mercy. It was obvious that he did not understand speech. Finally, Karapetyan left, telling the partisans to make up their own minds about what to do with the creature. He heard a few days later that the "wild man" had escaped. Obviously this story could have been an invention. But a report from the Ministry of the Interior in Daghestan confirmed its truth. The "wild man" had been court-martialled and executed as a deserter.

It was in January 1958 that Dr Alexander Pronin, of Leningrad University, reported seeing an Alma. He was in the Pamirs, and saw the creature outlined against a cliff-top. It was man-like, covered with reddish-grey hair, and he watched it for more than five minutes; three days later he saw it again at the same spot. For some reason good Marxists poured scorn on the notion of a "wild man"; but the evidence went on accumulating, until Boris Porshnev began to make an attempt to coordinate the sightings. The considerable body of evidence he has accumulated is described in some detail in Odette Tchernine's impressive book, *The Yeti*.

Wild Men

To summarize: the evidence for the existence of the Yeti, or Alma, or Bigfoot, or Sasquatch, is very strong indeed; hundreds of sightings make it unlikely that it is an invention. If we assume then for a moment that it really exists, what is it?

Dr Myra Shackley, lecturer in archaeology at Leicester University, believes she knows the answer. She is convinced that the Yeti is a Neanderthal man. And this is also the conclusion reached by Odette Tchernine on the basis of the Soviet evidence. Neanderthal man was the predecessor of modern man. He seems to have appeared first on earth about a hundred thousand years ago. He was smaller and more ape-like than modern man, with the well-known receding forehead and simian jaw. He lived in caves, and the piles of animal bones discovered in such caves suggest that Neanderthal woman was a sluttish housewife, and that his habitation must have stunk of rotting flesh. He was also a cannibal. But he was by no means a mere animal. Coloring pigments in Neanderthal caves suggest that he loved color; he certainly wove screens of colored flowers. And since he buried these with his dead, it seems certain that he believed in an afterlife. Mysterious round stones found in his habitations suggest that he was also a sun-worshipper.

Our ancestor, Cro-Magnon man, came on earth about fifty thousand years ago; it was he who made all the famous cave paintings. Neanderthal man vanished completely over the next twenty thousand years, and the mystery of his disappearance has never been solved. The general view is that he was exterminated by Cro-Magnon man (William Golding's novel *The Inheritors* is a story of the encounter between the two; so is H. G. Wells's earlier *The Grisly Men*).

The psychologist Stan Gooch advanced a startling thesis in his book *The Neanderthal Question* – that Neanderthals were not entirely exterminated, but that their women occasionally bore children to Cro-Magnon males. The descendants of these products of cross-breeding became the Jews. (It should be noted that Gooch is himself Jewish.) Gooch believes that Neanderthal man was more "psychic" than Cro-Magnon, and that such psychic faculties as present-day man now possesses are inherited from these Neanderthal ancestors.

Whether or not we can accept Gooch's theory, it seems reasonable to suppose that Neanderthal man may have survived, driven into the wilder and less hospitable places of the earth by his conqueror. Myra Shackley has travelled to the Altai mountains of Mongolia and collected evidence for the existence of Almas. "They live in caves, hunt for food, use stone tools, and wear animal skins and fur." And she mentions that in 1972 a Russian doctor met a family of Almas. In fact, Odette Tchernine cites a number of such stories. Professor Porshnev discovered again and again evidence among mountain people that they knew of the existence of "wild men"; the Abkhazians still have stories of how they drove the wild men out of the district they

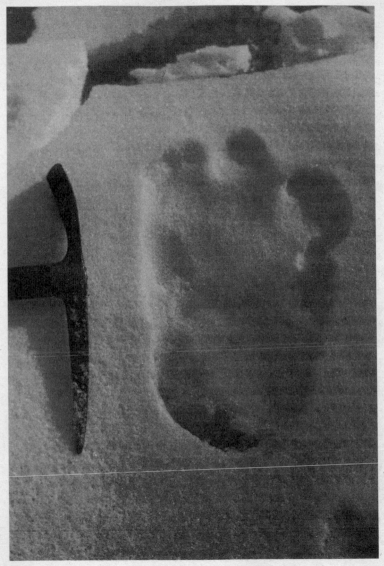

Yeti footprint found on a glacier in Nepal

colonized. Tchernine refers to these wild men as "pre-hominids".

Porshnev himself investigated a case of a female Alma who had been caught in the Ochamchir region in the mid-nineteenth century. Hunters captured a "wild woman" who had ape-like features and was covered in hair; for several years in captivity she was so violent that she could not be approached, and food had to be thrown to her. They called her Zana. Porshnev interviewed many old people – one was a hundred and five – who remembered Zana. They told him how she had become domesticated, and would perform simple tasks like grinding corn. She had a massive bosom, thick muscular arms and legs, and thick fingers; she could not endure warm rooms but preferred the cold. She loved to gorge herself on grapes in the vineyard, and also enjoyed wine – she would drink heavily then sleep for hours. This may explain how she became a mother on several occasions, to different fathers. Her children usually died because she washed them in the freezing river. (Presumably, having half-human characteristics, they lacked her tremendous inherited endurance of cold). Finally, her newborn children were taken away from her and they grew up among the people of the village. Unlike their mother, they could talk and were reasonable human beings. The youngest of these died as recently as 1954 (Zana died about 1890). Porshnev interviewed two of her grandchildren, and noted their dark skin and Negroid looks. Shalikula, the grandson, had such powerful jaws that he could pick up a chair with a man sitting on it. Here, it would seem, is solid, undeniable evidence of the existence of "wild men".

2

Fairies – the Original "Little Green Men"?

If alien creatures have actually contacted the human race, sceptics argue, why are reports of "little green men from Mars" confined almost entirely to the last hundred years? The folk myths of the pre-industrial age were full of fairies, pixies and elementals – now we are told of aliens, UFOs and apemen. Is it not likely that our twentieth-century, science-fiction goblins are also the product of too much imagination – or perhaps mental instability or alcohol?

Such an argument presupposes that all fairy stories are absurd and incredible, but can a scientific observer afford to be so wholesale? Most cultures throughout history have legends and stories of "the shining-ones" or their local elfin equivalent. Should we casually discount thousands of years of reported sightings, especially when reputable witnesses still claim to see fairies here in the modern age?

In the summer of 1897 the poet W. B. Yeats went to stay at Coole Park, Galway, Ireland, with Lady Augusta Gregory, who was to become his close friend and patroness, and the two of them began collecting fairy stories from the local peasantry. Yeats had already compiled two collections of Irish myths and fairy tales by interviewing peasants in his home county of Sligo. But he now came to recognize that the majority of Irish country folk accepted the existence of fairies, not as some kind of half-believed superstition – like touching wood – but as a concrete fact of life.

Yeats's father was a total skeptic, and Yeats himself had been inclined to toy with a belief in fairies as a kind of reaction to the materialism of the modern world – in short, as a kind of wishful thinking. His collaboration with Lady Gregory made him aware that belief in fairies could hardly be dismissed as wishful thinking. G. K. Chesterton, who met him several years later, was impressed by his insistence on the factual reality of fairies and wrote of Yeats in his autobiography,

> He was the real original rationalist who said that the fairies stand to reason. He staggered the materialists by attacking their abstract materialism with a completely concrete mysticism; "Imagination!" he would say with withering contempt; "There wasn't much imagination when Farmer Hogan was dragged out of bed and thrashed like a sack of potatoes – that they did, they had 'um out"; the Irish accent warming with scorn; "they had 'um out and thumped 'um; and that's not the sort of thing that a man wants to imagine."

Chesterton goes on to make a very important point,

> It is the fact that it is not abnormal men like artists, but normal men like peasants, who have borne witness a thousand times to such things; it is the farmers who see the fairies. It is the agricultural laborer who calls a spade a spade who also calls a spirit a spirit; it is the woodcutter with no axe to grind . . . who will say he saw a man hang on the gallows, and afterwards hang round it as a ghost.

A few years later Yeats was to encourage the orientalist W. Y. Evans Wentz – best known for his translation of the *Tibetan Book of the Dead* – to study the folklore of the fairies; the result was Wentz's first book, *The Fairy Faith in Celtic Countries* (1911), a bulky and scholarly volume based upon his own extensive fieldwork. Yeats's friend, the poet AE (George Russell), contributed an anonymous piece to the book (under the title "An Irish Mystic's Testimony") in which he described his own fairy sightings with the factual accuracy and precision of an anthropologist describing primitive tribes: shining beings, opalescent beings, water beings, wood beings, lower elementals:

> The first of [the fairies] I saw I remember very clearly . . . . there was first a dazzle of light, and then I saw that this came from the heart of a tall figure with a body apparently shaped out of half-transparent or opalescent air, and throughout the body ran a radiant electrical fire, to which the heart seemed the center. Around the head of this being and through its waving luminous hair, which was blown all about the body like living strands of gold, there appeared flaming wing-like auras. From the being itself light seemed to stream outwards in every direction; and the effect left on me after the vision was one of extraordinary lightness, joyousness or ecstasy.

Wentz concludes that the factual and scientific evidence for the existence of fairies is overwhelming, that in fact, "there are hundreds of proven cases of phenomena."

The Cottingley Fairies

But AE's fairies were essentially "visions" and could therefore be classified with unicorns or centaurs. In

25

1920, nine years after Wentz's book appeared, the British public was intrigued to learn of new scientific evidence that seemed to place belief in "the little people" on an altogether more solid foundation. The front cover of the Christmas issue of the *Strand* magazine announced: "An Epoch-Making Event . . . . Described by Conan Doyle." Facing the opening page of the article was a photograph of a teenage girl in a white cotton dress, sitting in a grassy field and holding out her hand to a dancing gnome. Another photograph showed a younger girl gazing mildly into the camera over a group of four cavorting fairies, complete with gossamer wings. The caption under the first photograph stated: "This picture and the even more extraordinary one of fairies on page 465 are the two most astounding photographs ever published. How they were taken is fully described in Sir A. Conan Doyle's article."

It was not a seasonal joke. Doyle and his fellow investigators were convinced that the two photographs virtually proved the existence of "the little people". The resulting controversy was to remain unsettled for the next sixty years.

The girls in the photograph were Elsie Wright and Frances Griffiths, and they lived in the village of Cottingley, in Yorkshire, England. They had taken the photographs three and a half years earlier, in the summer of 1917, and had consistently claimed, often in the face of extremely skeptical cross-examination, that the photographs were of real fairies.

The village of Cottingley is situated near Bradford, although it has today been swallowed up by suburbs. In 1917 it was surrounded by green English countryside. It was in April of that year that ten-year-old Frances

Griffiths had moved to the village with her mother, Annie, from South Africa; her father was fighting in France. She later claimed that she soon realized there were fairies in the fields around her home, especially near the local beck (stream), which ran down a steep-sided dell at the bottom of her garden. She later described the first time she said she had seen a fairy down by the stream.

One evening after school I went down to the beck to a favorite place – the willow overhanging the stream . . . . then a willow leaf started shaking violently – just one. I'd seen it happen before – there was no wind, and it was odd that one leaf should shake . . . . as I watched, a small man, all dressed in green, stood on the branch with the stem of the leaf in his hand, which he seemed to be shaking at something he was looking at. I daren't move for fear of frightening him. He looked straight at me and disappeared.

But she had decided not to tell anyone for fear of being laughed at.

She explained how, as the summer wore on, she had become increasingly fascinated by the stream and how she would spend hours "fairy-watching" in the dell. She occasionally missed her footing on the slippery bank and landed up to her waist in the water. When she returned home her mother would slap her and make her promise not to go near the stream, but Frances never kept her promise – she could not resist the urge to see the fairies.

One day, when she arrived home soaked yet again, her mother and her Aunt Polly pressed hard for an explanation. What they heard left them both slightly breathless: "I go to see the fairies! That's why – to see the fairies!"

At this point, to the surprise of the two women,

Frances's cousin, seventeen-year-old Elsie Wright, came to her defense and insisted that she, too, had seen fairies. No amount of questioning could shake the girls' story. According to Doyle's article, it was this confrontation that convinced the two cousins that they must produce some indisputable evidence to make the grown-ups eat their words.

That is why, on a Saturday afternoon in July 1917, Elsie asked her father, Arthur Wright, if she could borrow his plate camera. He was understandably reluctant, since the camera was new and the plates expensive, but he eventually gave way. The girls hurried off to the stream and were back in half an hour. After tea Arthur was coaxed into developing the plate.

As the plate started to develop, he realized that it was a picture of Frances leaning on a bank that seemed to be scattered with sandwich papers. Then, to his amazement, he saw that the "papers" were tiny human forms with wings growing from their backs; they were apparently four dancing fairies.

The girls' mothers didn't know what to think. Both had recently become interested in Theosophy – the movement founded by Madame Blavatsky, who taught that behind the solid world of everyday reality there was an invisible world peopled with spiritual beings, including nature spirits or fairies. In theory, at any rate, they agreed.

Arthur Wright, on the other hand, was skeptical:

"You've been up to summat."

"No we haven't," Elsie insisted.

He knew that Elsie was a gifted artist and was convinced that the fairies were paper cutouts – although a search of the girls' room and the wastebaskets failed to turn up any snippets of paper left over from manufactured fairies. And in spite of all their protestations, he remained unconvinced. Eventually, the matter was dropped. But in August the girls borrowed the camera again; this time they returned with a picture of Elsie sitting in a field watching a dancing gnome. They explained that they often saw gnomes in the field just above the stream. After this, in the interest of peace and quiet, Arthur Wright refused further loans of his camera. But several prints were made of each plate.

The whole affair might have been forgotten if it had not been for the Theosophical Society. After the war, with its appalling casualties, Spiritualism and Theosophy had made thousands of new converts, and the Bradford Unity Hall, where the Society held its meetings, was always packed.

After a meeting in which fairies had been mentioned, Polly Wright approached the speaker and told him about the photographs. He asked to see them and copies were soon circulating among the Bradford Theosophists.

Shortly afterward Polly Wright received a letter from Edward L. Gardner, head of the Theosophist Lodge in London; he was excited about the photographs and asked to see the original prints and negatives. Upon receiving the negatives, Gardner had them copied and the copies then retouched. He was quite open about this. In a letter to Doyle he wrote,

> I begged the loan of the actual negatives – and two quarter plates came by post a few days after. One was a fairly clear one, the other much under exposed . . . . the immediate upshot was that a positive was taken from each negative, that the originals might be preserved untouched, and then new negatives were prepared and intensified to serve as better printing mediums.

29

He then took the original prints and negatives to a professional photographer, Harold Snelling. Snelling's previous employer had assured Gardner that "what Snelling doesn't know about faked photography isn't worth knowing."

It was Snelling who examined the four dancing fairies negative (the better-exposed plate). He reported to Gardner,

> This plate is a single exposure . . . . These dancing fairies are not made of paper nor of any fabric; they are not painted on a photographed background – but what gets me most is that all these figures have *moved* during exposure.

Gardner, delighted with this verdict, began showing lantern slides of the photographs at Theosophy meetings around the country. And in the summer of 1920 he was flattered to receive a letter from the creator of Sherlock Holmes.

The sixty-year-old Doyle was not a Theosophist, but in recent years he had become convinced of the truth of Spiritualism. He had already been commissioned by the *Strand* to write an article on fairies, and the news of the Cottingley photographs must have sounded like a gift from the beyond. When he saw the photographs, Doyle was at first skeptical about them. But a meeting with Gardner convinced him that they could be genuine. The next step obviously, was to try to obtain more of them.

Toward the end of July 1920, Edward Gardner went to visit the Wrights for the first time – Frances was then in Scarborough with her father and so was not present. Elsie's father made no attempt to conceal the fact that he was unhappy about the whole situation. He still felt that the photographs were fakes, and the high esteem in which he held Doyle had declined sharply when he heard that Doyle was now convinced "by our Elsie, and her at the bottom of her class!"

Some have thought it strange that Sir Arthur Conan Doyle – inventor of Sherlock Holmes, the archetypal pragmatic investigator – should have also championed the reality of fairies. In fact Doyle remained a strong believer in the supernatural all his life. For example, his Professor Challenger novel *The Land of Mist* was effectively an evangelistic treatise for the spiritualist movement. The belief in "unseen forces" seems to have been a very important aspect of the author's life, even if his most famous fictional character always rejected the supernatural out-of-hand.

Biographical researchers have suggested that this paradox in Conan Doyle's outlook sprang from two of the major influences from his youth. On one side, he was trained as a doctor and man of science, on the other was the fact that his father died insane, claiming to the end that he could see fairies . . . .

But his wife had a long and thoughtful talk with Gardner, and Elsie later showed him the field, and the spot by the stream where the photographs had been taken. Some people had felt that the stream photograph looked a little too "magical" to be true, with its little toadstools and waterfall; Gardner was delighted to find that it looked exactly as in the photograph. He reported to Doyle that he was convinced that the girls were genuine. Doyle still felt that more photographs were needed to prove the case. So, as Doyle embarked on a steamship south to Australia to lecture on Spiritualism, Gardner went north again, this time armed with new cameras and two dozen carefully numbered plates. (Oddly enough, nobody bothered to note how many plates were eventually used by the girls, so the numbering was wasted).

On this occasion Gardner also met Frances, then fourteen, who had returned from Scarborough for the summer holidays. He soon formed the conviction that both girls were psychic. Since the weather was rainy and dull – bad visibility for fairy-spotting, according to the girls – he left the cameras behind and returned to London. The rain continued for the next two weeks.

The morning of August 19 was dull and misty, but when it brightened up later, the girls decided to try out the cameras. They returned with two more photographs, which were promptly developed by the unbelieving Arthur Wright. One was of a winged fairy, with stylish-looking bobbed hair, standing placidly on a branch, offering Elsie a tiny bunch of harebells. The other was of a slightly blurred Frances jerking her head back as another winged fairy leapt toward her. It was clear that it was leaping rather than flying because the wings were unblurred by movement. Gardner later had these photographs examined by an expert, who again reported that they showed no signs of fraud.

The last photograph was taken on a drizzly day, August 21, 1920. Later referred to by Frances as a "fairy sunbath," it seems to show two fairies hanging a gossamerlike material over a tuft of grass, to make a shelter or suntrap. Frances said she often saw the little people doing this on dull days, as if to keep themselves warm. Oddly enough, this phenomenon has been reported in various unconnected fairy sightings before and after the Cottingley photographs. The fairies in this last photograph have a semi-transparent quality, which detractors claimed was a sign of double exposure but which believers ascribed to the effect of cold on the fairy constitution.

Since Doyle had written the *Strand* article before he left for Australia, it made no reference to these last three photographs. Even so, when the magazine was published that Christmas – with retouched, much sharper prints – it caused a sensation. The Cottingley fairies became the talk of every London dinner table. But skeptics were outraged at what they regarded as the public's infantile gullibility. Their basic argument was summed up in the January 5 issue of *Truth* "For the true explanation of these fairy photographs what is wanted is not a knowledge of occult phenomena but a knowledge of children."

One detractor, a doctor by the name of Major Hall-Edwards, even went so far as to say,

> I criticize the attitude of those who declared there is something supernatural in the circumstances attending to the taking of these pictures because, as a medical man, I believe that the inculcation of such absurd ideas into the minds of children will result in later life in manifestations of nervous disorder and mental disturbances.

(One wonders how he felt about parents telling their children that Santa Claus was a real person.)

On the other hand, the Cottingley fairies had their supporters in the media. The *South Wales Argus* commented, "The day we kill our Santa Claus with our statistics we shall have plunged a glorious world into deepest darkness." The *City News* said more pragmatically, "It seems at this point that we must either believe in the almost incredible mystery of the fairy or in the almost incredible wonders of faked photographs."

Doyle himself, still in Australia, was delighted by the new pictures. He wrote to Gardner,

> My heart gladdened when out here in far Australia I had your note and the photographs, which are confirmatory of our published results. When our fairies are admitted other psychic phenomena will find a more ready acceptance . . . . we have had continued messages at séances for some time that a visible sign was coming through.

In March 1921, three months after the first article, the *Strand* published Doyle's second, illustrated with the new photographs. The reaction was much as before – one major criticism being that the dresses and hairstyles looked too contemporary. Other critics objected that the fairies looked *too* much like typical "storybook" fairies. Defenders suggested that the physical appearance of the fairies might be an ectoplasmic projection based on what the spirits thought was expected of them. And since Elsie and Frances were interested in contemporary fashions, their fairies might well look like a strange hybrid of the two elements.

As the photographs were reproduced in foreign publications, and the debate spread overseas, it became more heated. But the second set of photographs failed to tip the balance. Few people felt that they made any real difference.

One basic problem was that both girls were minors, and as such their testimony was legally inadmissible; their parents were also unable to offer proof since they had never claimed to have seen any "little people." A photograph taken by an adult who could swear under oath that no trickery had been used might have been enough to swing the debate.

A friend of Doyle's, the psychic Geoffrey Hodson – who also claimed to have seen fairies – went to Cottingley to see what he could find out. Hodson arrived in Cottingley with his wife and Edward Gardner in August 1921. Gardner stayed for just over a week, during which the weather was generally poor and no fairies were seen. On the day before he left, both Hodson and the girls claimed to have sighted many "nature spirits" (as Hodson called them in his notebook), but failed to get any pictures. Hodson and his wife stayed on, and the fairy sightings became more frequent; but he still failed to capture any of them with a camera. In the end he admitted defeat and left.

At this point the debate ran out of steam; there seemed to be too little evidence to prove the case either way. In 1922 Doyle published a book entitled *The Coming of the Fairies*, but although it contained many photographs and reported fairy sightings, it failed to convince the skeptics. For the next forty years or so Elsie and Frances were forgotten.

In 1965 Elsie, then in her sixties, was tracked down in the Midlands by a *Daily Express* reporter, Peter Chambers. He believed that the pictures were faked, and Elsie's comment that people should be left to make up their own minds on the subject only deepened his skepticism. Elsie made the curious remark, "As for the photographs, let's say they are pictures of figments of our imagination, Frances's and mine, and leave it at that."

This might be taken in one of two ways – either she was making an oblique reference to the ectoplasm theory; or she was admitting that the fairies never existed outside her imagination. Now that the subject had been revived, there were many more interviews with both Frances and Elsie. Much was made of a new admission that they had seen *no* fairies during the visit of Geoffrey Hodson; they explained that they were thoroughly bored by the whole subject and felt him to be a fraud, so they amused themselves by pretending to see fairies and were maliciously amused when he said he could see them too. (In his own book on fairies Hodson insists that he *did* see "little people" at Cottingley.)

In 1971 Elsie was asked by the BBC's "Nationwide" program if her father had had a hand in the taking of the photographs. She replied, "I would swear on the Bible that father didn't know what was going on." But when asked if she would swear on the Bible that the photographs were not tricks, she replied after a pause, "I'd rather leave that open if you don't mind . . . . but my father had nothing to do with it, I can promise you that." Again she seemed to be close to admitting that there was some kind of fraud.

On the other hand, when Frances was asked by Yorkshire Television if the photographs were fabricated, she replied, "Of course not. You tell us how she could do it – remember she was sixteen and I was ten. Now then, as a child of ten, can you go through life and keep a secret?"

This, it seemed, was the chief argument in favor of the fairy photographs – that it seemed unlikely that Frances and Elsie would and could keep such a secret for so long.

Frances made this comment in 1976; the occasion was a television program about Frances and Elsie, which had been suggested by the Yorkshire psychical investigator

Joe Cooper. That is why, on September 10, 1976, the two women turned up at a house on Main Street, Cottingley, opposite the house where the Wright family had lived half a century earlier. In the intervening years, Elsie had lived in India with her husband, Frank Hill, a Scottish engineer; Frances had married a soldier, Frank Way, and had spent much time with him abroad.

Cooper describes Frances as "a bespectacled woman of middle class and height wearing fashionable denim clothes but with a dash of red and black about the scarf and blouse." Elsie, when she arrived, looked a good ten years younger than her seventy-five summers, dressed in fashionable slacks and "mod" gear, including a black derby hat. During the day Cooper became friendly with the two women, even carrying Elsie over a stile. The camera team interviewed locals – who all expressed extreme skepticism about the photographs – and filmed the women down by the stream. Interviewer Austin Mitchell made no secret of believing that the case of the Cottingley fairies had started as a joke, but had gotten out of hand. Cooper was inclined to believe Frances and Elsie. On camera, Elsie and Frances identified the place where they had seen a gnome and flatly denied that they had fabricated the photographs. When interviewed by Mitchell, Cooper stated his view that the girls had seen an "elemental form of fairy life" – that is to say, "nature spirits." After all, he noted, W. B. Yeats and thousands of his fellow countrymen were quite certain about the existence of fairies.

In 1977 there was an interesting development. A researcher named Fred Gettings, working on nine-teenth-century fairy illustrations, came upon *Princess Mary's Gift Book*, published during the First World War to make money for the Work for Women fund. It contained a poem entitled "A Spell for a Fairy" by Alfred Noyes, illustrated by Claude Shepperson. Two of the fairies in the illustration were virtually identical to the fairies in the first Cottingley photograph, which showed Frances gazing over the heads of five prancing sprites. Their positions had merely been reversed.

In August 1978, *The New Scientist* reported that the magician James Randi ("the Amazing Randi") and the Committee for the Scientific Investigation of Claims of the Paranormal (CSICOP) had put the photographs through an image-enhancement process and found that this revealed strings holding up the fairies. When Cooper told Elsie about the article she merely laughed and pointed out that there was nowhere in the region of the stream where string could have been tied. After a TV play about the fairies had been broadcast in October 1978, Randi expressed indignation that the BBC had failed to state clearly that the photographs had been proved to be fakes.

In 1981 Cooper was writing a book on telepathy and had some correspondence with Frances – who now lived in Ramsgate – about the subject. In September 1981 she asked him to come see her, telling him that there were "some things he should know." When he arrived she was still not ready to specify what these were. But the following day she asked him to drive her to Canterbury; once there, she asked him to wait for her while she went into the cathedral. When she returned they sat in a coffee shop, and she asked him what he thought of the first fairy photograph. He commented that it had been greatly touched up. Then Frances dropped her bombshell,

"From where I was, I could see the hatpins holding up

the figures. I've always marveled that anybody ever took it seriously."

"Why are you telling me?" asked the flabbergasted investigator.

"Because Elsie has already told Glenn" [Elsie's son].

"What about the other four? Are they fakes?"

Her answer was, in its way, as astonishing as the original admission, "Three of them. The last one's genuine."

Cooper and Frances now discussed writing a book together and giving Elsie a share of the proceeds; Frances was adamant that Elsie should play no part in writing the book. Cooper went to London to talk to his publisher. Unfortunately, the publisher was not particularly interested in a sixty-year-old story about fairies, especially since it ended so anticlimactically.

It was at this time the author and paranormal researcher Colin Wilson became involved in the story.

"I had met Joe Cooper at a weekend conference on parapsychology (at the Swanwick Conference Centre in Derbyshire) in 1980, and he had told me he had written a book on the Cottingley fairies – this, of course, was a year before Frances told him the true story. He sent me the manuscript, and I found it fascinating. I had also come across people – one of them a hardheaded Scottish TV interviewer – who claimed to have seen fairies, and I was simply not willing to rule out the possibility that "nature spirits" might exist. Joe's own research into the paranormal had convinced him that "elementals" could not merely be ruled out as an absurdity.

"In fact, I was on my way to Yorkshire to research a poltergeist haunting in Pontefract, and that weekend was something of a turning point in my life, for just before I left the conference center I met Guy Lyon Playfair, a psychical researcher with whom I had been in correspondence for some time. At this time I accepted the view of most people involved in psychical research – that poltergeists were a strange manifestation of the unconscious mind of a psychologically disturbed teenager. What Playfair suggested left me rather bewildered. He felt that while some poltergeists may be "spontaneous psychokinesis," mind over matter, the majority are genuine spirits who draw their energy from human beings, particularly children on the verge of puberty.

"I have described in my book *Poltergeist* how my visit to the Pritchard household in Pontefract soon convinced me that Guy Playfair knew what he was talking about. When Diane Pritchard, who had been the focus of the disturbances (ie, the person whose energy was "stolen" by the poltergeist), described how she was dragged up the stairs by some unknown force, I suddenly knew beyond all doubt that the poltergeist was *not* some manifestation of her own unconscious mind. It was a spirit. This meant that as a writer on the paranormal, I had to get off the fence and stop keeping an "open mind" about whether such things as spirits can exist.

"It seemed clear to me that the spirits involved in most poltergeist cases are those of the dead – in the Pontefract case, possibly that of a Cluniac monk who had been hanged for rape in the time of Henry VIII. (The gallows had been on the site of the Pritchard house.) But that did not necessarily mean that no other kinds of spirits can exist. The travel writer Laurens Van der Post, for example, had no doubt whatsoever that the "nature spirits" or gods of the Kalahari bushmen are real and can cause all kinds of problems. In *The Lost World of the Kalahari* he describes how "the spirits of the Slippery Hills" became offended when one of his team killed a warthog on their territory and caused endless mishaps until they received a proper apology. In *Poltergeist* I cited many similar stories. So it was hardly logical for me to deny the existence of "nature spirits" on the grounds that only a child could believe in them.

"But the problem with Joe Cooper's book, even in its original version, was that the story was too slight – it could be told in fifty pages, which seemed to mean that the rest had to be some kind of "padding." And since, at that point, both Frances and Elsie were still insisting that the photographs were genuine, the story had no real conclusion. I tried to find a publisher for the book but was unsuccessful. And at this point Joe said he wanted to rewrite it anyway; and there the matter rested.

"It was in the following year that Frances finally "came clean." Oddly enough, Joe was excited that the case had finally reached a definite conclusion. When he told me about Frances's confession, I was less optimistic. If the book ended with an admission of fraud, it would be an anticlimax.

"Joe Cooper came to the same conclusion. Late in 1982 an anthology called *The Unexplained*, of which I was a consulting editor, published his article "Cottingley: At Last the Truth," in which he revealed that the fairies in the first four photographs were cutouts stuck to the branches with hatpins. Understandably, this upset both Frances and Elsie. When Frances called Joe's wife on New Year's Day 1983, and Joe answered the phone, she called him a traitor and hung up. She died in 1986. Elsie died in 1988, maintaining to the end that she did not believe in fairies."

Which seems to be the end of the story . . . .

Or is it? Certainly the skeptics are justified in regarding the case as closed. Possibly they are correct. Yet before we make up our minds, there are a few interesting points to be made.

What Frances is asking us to believe is this: she came to England from South Africa in 1917 when she was ten, and went to stay with her sixteen-year-old cousin, Elsie, in Cottingley. Elsie claimed to have had some odd ghostly experiences. For example, she insisted that when she was four she was regularly visited in bed by a woman who wore a tight dress buttoned up to her neck. And when she was six she woke up one night and called for a drink; when no one replied, she went downstairs and found a strange man and woman in the house. She asked where her parents were and was told they had gone out to play cards with the neighbors. Elsie said she wanted to go and find them, and the man opened the front door and let her out. Her parents – who were, in fact, playing cards with the neighbors – were startled to see her and even more startled to hear about the man and woman, for they had left the house empty. But when they went to investigate, the house *was* empty.

Frances had had no "psychic" experiences. But in the spring of 1918 she saw her first gnome. She had gone down to the stream after school and observed a phenomenon she had often observed before: a single willow leaf began to shake on the tree by the stream. Then a small man, all dressed in green, was standing on the branch. Frances watched, breathless, terrified of disturbing him. The little man looked straight at her, then disappeared. After that, she claimed, she often saw little men wearing coats of grayish green and matching caps by the stream. She gradually reached the conclusion that the little men were engaged in some kind of purposeful activity, perhaps associated with helping plants to grow. Later, she began to see fairies, with and without wings. These were smaller than the elves; they had white faces and arms and often seemed to be holding some kind of meeting. Elsie, she insists, never saw the fairies or little men.

It was after falling into the stream yet again that Frances admitted that she went there to see fairies. And it was the total skepticism of the adults that led Elsie to decide to take some fairy photographs. This was not simply a desire to deceive. Elsie believed Frances when she said she saw fairies; her own psychic experiences made it seem quite plausible. She wanted to shake the credulity of the grown-ups. So the photographs were taken with cutouts propped up by hatpins.

When the world suddenly became interested in the fairies, the girls were in a difficult position. The photographs were fakes, yet – according to the girls – the fairies really existed. If the whole thing had been a hoax, it would have been easier to confess. But it was not a hoax – not totally, anyway. They were in an embarrassing and anomalous position. If they admitted that the photographs were fakes, they would be implying that the whole affair was a deception. And that would be as untrue as continuing to maintain that the photographs were genuine. So they decided to keep silent.

Then the whole affair blew up again in 1965, the situation was unchanged. It is true that Elsie, now a hardheaded woman in her sixties, was no longer convinced that Frances had seen fairies; yet she was absolutely certain that *she* had had "psychic" experiences and was therefore prepared to be open-minded. As to Frances, she *had* seen fairies and had nothing to retract. In a letter to Leslie Gardner, the son of Edward Gardner, Elsie remarked that after her interview with Peter Chambers (in 1965), in which she had declared that people must judge for themselves and that the pictures were "figments of our imaginations," Frances had said indignantly, "What did you say that for? You know very well that they were real."

In fact, Frances had always maintained that the fairies were real. In November 1918 she sent the first fairy photograph to a friend in South Africa and scrawled on the back: "Elsie and I are very friendly with the beck Fairies. It's funny I never used to see them in Africa. It must be too hot for them there."

Other Sightings

In his original manuscript of the Cottingley book, Joe Cooper had included a chapter entitled "Other Sightings", consisting of accounts of fairies related to him by various witnesses, and it makes clear why he believed Frances. One man, a healer, told how he was sitting with a girl in Gibraltar, eating a sandwich, when it was snatched from him by "a little man about eighteen inches high." An eighty-year-old official of the Theosophical Society insisted that when he was a small boy he was often visited in bed by a green-clad gnome. Another old man described seeing a green-clad gnome, about two feet high, walking along a path in a cornfield. Some young male students told how, when walking in a wood near Bradford, they saw fairies who were "circling and dancing" but who were invisible to the direct gaze; they could only be seen "out of the corner of the eye." An elderly woman showed Cooper a photograph of a gnome seen through a frosty window; she claimed that she had come down one morning, seen the gnome, and rushed upstairs to get her camera. The photograph also shows diminutive white rabbits.

Joe Cooper finally published most of these accounts in his book *Modern Psychic Experiences*, together with many more. A New Zealand medium named Dorothy described how she used to play with a "spirit" girl named Mabel as a child and how she had first seen fairies who came from under plants. One day she came home to find her father unconscious on the floor – a gastric ulcer had perforated – and the fairies took charge and escorted her to the doctor's house. Joe Cooper's own niece, Jo, who was in her thirties, described how, at the age of sixteen, she had seen three little men crouching on top of a wall.

If like Joe Cooper, investigators decide to suspend their natural incredulity, they will find an impressive number of reported fairy sightings in the twentieth century. In 1936, the popular English literary weekly, *John O'London's*, invited and published a series of letters from readers who believed they had met the little people. By that time, over sixteen years after the publication of the Cottingley photographs, the whole fairy issue was generally considered silly and old-hat by the British public, yet many apparently serious, sensible people risked ridicule to tell their bizarre tales.

Most of the stories were simple and down-to-earth: witnesses claimed to have seen gnomes standing by the side of the road as they drove past, or to have spotted tiny but seemingly solid people in their gardens or quiet countryside areas. The sprites rarely seemed to be doing anything extraordinary. They tended to be sunbathing, taking in the view or harvesting berries. While some witnesses claimed to have encountered fairies decades before – often when they were children – a number claimed to have seen them as recently as that same year. All in all, the reader is left with the impression that most of the witnesses were not seeking to impress, but were simply relaying an event that thoroughly baffled them.

The bewilderment of fairy witnesses is quite understandable – their common sense has received a direct blow from the evidence of their own eyes. A necessary part of adulthood is to "put away childish things", but what if they refuse to be put away? A meeting with Rumplestiltskin shakes even those who accept other paranormal phenomena such as ghosts, ESP and alien abduction.

In her biography, *Witch Among Us*, the psychic Lois Bourne tells of seeing a pixie while she was staying in a cottage in Crantock, Cornwall. During a visit one evening, Rob, the husband of one of Lois's friends, asked if she would like to see a goblin. He explained that one appeared among the rushes of the millstream of Treago Mill, Cuberts Heath, every morning at sunrise. The next morning Lois and her husband Wilfred joined Rob at the mill gate and crept with him up-stream. Bourne writes,

> I have never been able to decide, and still cannot decide, whether I really saw that goblin, or if Rob made me see it . . . . Whatever it was, there, sitting on a stone calmly washing his socks, was an elfin creature with a red hat, green coat and trews, one yellow sock on, and one in his tiny hands in the process of being washed. I

remember thinking at the time, in my sleepy, be-
fuddled, but practical way, "What an atrocious color
combination." Suddenly he saw us and he disappeared
. . . . "Now do you believe me?" asked Rob.

Bourne claimed that all three of them saw the tiny, sock-
washing creature, so it could not have been a simple
hallucination.

The many other psychic experiences related in Bourne's
book are rather less fantastic, which leads to an obvious
question – if she did invent some or all of the stories, why
discredit her efforts with a silly and unbelievable lie about
goblins? As with many paranormal reports, the unbiased
observer seems left with only three possibilities – that the
witness was bizarrely mistaken, that they are an incredible
liar, or that they are telling the truth!

An author on psychic phenomena, Marc Alexander,
tells an interesting story that adds a scientific twist to the
hunt for fairies. A friend of his, New Zealander Pat
Andrew, told him that he remembered meeting a pixie
when he was six-years-old. Alexander suggested they try
hypnotism to "regress" Andrew back to the encounter.
(Hypnotic regression allows access to memories inacces-
sible to the conscious mind. The memory experiences
are so full and intense the hypnotic subjects actually
believe themselves to be back in the past. It is a method
often used by psychiatrists on patients and, occasionally,
by the police medicos on witnesses with memory block-
age.) The result was an amazing one-sided conversation
that left Alexander with no doubt that, whether the
young Andrew had really seen a pixie or not, he undoubtedly believed that he had.

Of course, seeing may not always be believing; we can

be subject to all kinds of visual deceptions and illusions. Most people will see a mirage or experience other sensory delusions at some time in their lives – anything from the shimmering of non-existent water to full-blown hallucinations – but, generally, when they blink, change position or have a lie-down out of the sun, the delusion will vanish. A striking element in many fairy sighting is the witness's certainty that whatever they saw, it was *not* just a trick of the light. But could they be tricks of the mind?

A major objection raised by skeptics is the near total lack of physical evidence for fairies, extraterrestrials, Yetis and all the other fantastic animals of ancient and modern legend. The reason for this, they say, is that these are no more than creatures of the imagination. This will be cold comfort to anyone who has been on the receiving end of poltergeist mischief, found their crops flattened in bizarre patterns or their livestock hideously mutilated with no evidence that points to a human agency. Some parapsychologists have suggested a third possibility: that fairies are just the European projection of the "spirits" believed in by cultures around the globe. These are not just creatures of the imagination, nor actual physical beings, yet they do seem to be able to influence our minds and surroundings. In the next chapter we will look more closely at the theory that we may share the world with non-corporeal aliens.

3

The Gray Man of Ben MacDhui

The fairies and little people considered in the last chapter, generally show an indifferent attitude to human observers. Other "visitors", however, are less friendly. In traditional folktales the world over, supernatural beings often seem bent on the malicious destruction of any human that crosses their path. Is this the superstitious fear of the ignorant peasant or an understanding of strange forces which modern man ignores or discounts as madness when he meets them?

The lone mountaineer in the Scottish Cairngorms is as isolated from the modern day as an Amazonian shaman or a Kalahari Bushman. If alien, supernatural entities do haunt our world, the lonely slopes of Ben MacDhui are as likely a stamping ground as the deep jungle or the arid veldt.

At the 27th Annual General Meeting of the Cairngorm Club in Aberdeen in December 1925, the eminent mountaineer Professor Norman Collie made a startling disclosure. He told how in 1890 he was climbing alone on Ben MacDhui, 4,000 feet above sea level, when he had a terrifying experience. As he was returning from the cairn on the plateau, there was a heavy mist and Collie heard crunching noises behind him "as if someone was walking after me, but taking steps three or four times the length of my own." He told himself it was nonsense, but

49

as he walked on, and the footsteps continued to sound behind him, "I was seized with terror and took to my heels, staggering blindly among the boulders for four or five miles down to Rothiemurchus Forest."

In fact Collie had told the story twenty-three years earlier to friends in New Zealand, and the result was a report in a New Zealand newspaper headlined: "A Professor's Panic." As a result of this story, another Scottish mountaineer, Dr A. M. Kellas – who was to die during the Mount Everest Reconnaissance expedition of 1921–2 – wrote to Collie telling him of his own curious experience on Ben MacDhui. Kellas and his brother Henry had been chipping the rock for crystals late one afternoon when they saw a giant figure coming down towards them from the cairn. It passed out of sight briefly in a dip, and as the two men fled down the mountainside again in mist, both of them were convinced that they were being followed by the "giant".

This account makes it sound as if some form of "Yeti", or Abominable Snowman, lives on the slopes of Ben MacDhui. But accounts by other climbers make it clear that the explanation may not be as simple as this. Peter Densham, who was in charge of aeroplane rescue work in the Cairngorms during the Second World War, described in an interview with a journalist how in May 1945 he had left the village of Aviemore and climbed to the cairn on the summit. Suddenly, as he was looking at the distant peak of Ben Nevis, the mist closed in. He sat there eating chocolate, conscious of strange noises which he attributed to the expansion and contraction of the rocks, when he had a strong feeling that there was someone near him. Then he felt something cold on the back of his neck, and a sense of pressure. He stood up, and heard crunching noises from the direction of the cairn. He went towards the cairn to investigate, "not in the least frightened." Then suddenly he experienced a feeling of apprehension, and found himself running towards Lurcher's Crag, with its sheer drop. "I tried to stop myself and found this was extremely difficult to do. It was as if someone was pushing me. I managed to deflect my course, but with a great deal of difficulty . . . ." He ran most of the way back down the mountain.

On another occasion Densham was on the mountain with his friend Richard Frere, searching for an aeroplane that was reported to have crashed. They were sitting close to the cairn when Densham was surprised to hear Frere apparently talking to himself on the other side of the cairn. Then he realized that Frere was talking to someone else. "I went round and found myself joining in the conversation. It was a strange experience which seemed to have a psychic aspect. We talked to someone invisible for some time, and it seemed we had carried on this conversation for some little time when we suddenly realized that there was no one there but ourselves. Afterwards, neither of us, strangely, could recall the purport of this extraordinary conversation." What seems even stranger is that when Frere himself was tracked down by Affleck Gray, the author of a book called *The Big Gray Man of Ben MacDhui*, he had no recollection of the episode described by Densham. But he had had his own strange experiences on the mountain, and described it to Gray as "the most mysterious mountain I have ever been on." He told Gray of a day when he had climbed to the high pass of Lairig Ghru, above Ben MacDhui, and sat gazing down on the cliffs of Lurcher's Crag with its cascade of water. Then he found himself slipping into a "weird and disagreeable" train of thought, so he stood up and walked. But the gloom turned to a sense of deep depression and apathy. Then suddenly he became certain that he was not alone. "Very close to me, permeating the air which moved so softly in the summer's wind, there was a Presence, utterly abstract but intensely real." Then Frere noticed something else. "The silence of the mountain was violated by an intensely high singing note, a sound which was just within the aural capacity, which never rose or fell .... The sound, it seemed, was coming from the very soil of the mountains." This sound continued until he was below Lurcher's Crag, when the music became so faint that he was not sure whether it was there at all. But the "abstract Presence" seemed to cling to him "with some sort of desperate eagerness as if it passionately desired to leave the mountain which it haunted . . . ." Then there was a momentary flash of terror, and it was gone.

The experience of the strange, sustained note is not as unusual as Frere apparently thought. In her autobiography *The Infinite Hive*, the eminent psychical investigator Rosalind Heywood calls it "the Singing". She describes it as "a kind of continuous vibrant inner *quasi*-sound, to which the nearest analogy is the noise induced by pressing a seashell against the ear, or perhaps the hum of a distant dynamo." Rosalind Heywood could hear "the Singing" fairly constantly – although very faintly – if she switched her full attention to it. She says that "it is far more evident in some places than in others; particularly so in a quiet wood, for instance, or on a moor or a mountain . . . ." She notes that she also hears it in churches and college libraries, "places where thought or devotion have been intense for years." She finds that "mountain Singing conveys a different 'atmosphere' from church Singing, as an oboe conveys a different 'atmosphere' from a trumpet." And she says that she has met four other people who have heard it. In one case, she mentioned it to a young engineer, convinced that he was a thorough pragmatist; to her surprise, he replied, "Oh yes, I hear that too, in places where there have just been strong emotions." So to some extent the "Singing" seems to be a kind of "recording": Rosalind Heywood says that she can also "feel" it when she goes into a room where intense thought has been going on. Yet it cannot be wholly due to human "vibrations", since she mentions that the Hampstead tube station – the deepest in London – is the only place where she has not heard it. "The silence was dead."

If "the Singing" can be heard in places where intense thought or worship has taken place, this verifies that it could be regarded as some kind of "recording". In the 1840s an American professor of anatomy named Joseph Rodes Buchanan came to the interesting conclusion that every object has its own history somehow "imprinted" on it, and that "psychics" can sense this history by holding it in their hands; he called this faculty "psychometry". He observed that handwritten letters seem to be particularly good "recorders" of the writer's state of mind, particularly if the writer was feeling some powerful emotion at the time. In the early twentieth century, the scientist and psychical researcher Sir Oliver Lodge advanced the theory that "ghosts" may be "recordings" – that the powerful emotions associated with some tragedy may be imprinted on the walls of the room in which it has taken place, so that a "sensitive" person who walked into the room would have a strange feeling of misery and oppression, or perhaps even see the tragedy reenacted. A Cambridge don named Tom Lethbridge suggested a very similar "tape recording" theory half a century later. Lethbridge suggested that these "recordings" are imprinted on some kind of electrical field, and he believed that mountains, deserts and woodlands each have their own special type of "field". (He seemed to feel that the field of water is the best "recorder", so that ghosts are often associated with damp places.)

It seems conceivable, then, that when Rosalind Heywood heard "the Singing" she was simply picking up some kind of electrical field – a field which, on account of its properties, we might christen "the psychic field". Why Richard Frere should suddenly have become aware of this field on the slopes of Ben MacDhui must remain an open question. But at least it seems to offer some kind of confirmation that his feeling of menace and depression was not merely imagination.

The episode in which Frere and Densham held a conversation with some invisible entity seems even stranger; presumably they were responding to some "presence" on a subconscious level, almost as if dreaming. This could also explain why Frere could not even remember the episode later. Frere also told Affleck Gray a curious story about a friend – whose identity he was not at liberty to disclose – who decided to spend the night on Ben MacDhui to win a bet. He set up his tent by the summit cairn on a January night. (This is not a manmade cairn, but a natural formation eroded by the weather). He also began to experience the familiar sense of unreality, and "the morbidly analytical directioning of thought." Frere explained: "He did not feel in any way mad: the terror which possessed him concerned the imminent impact of knowledge which he knew would always set him aside from his fellows. It was as if he was the unwilling recipient of a vast range of new revolutionary thought impulses built up in some all-powerful mind. And the mind was neither human nor anti-human; it just had nothing to do with him at all."

He fell asleep and woke up "to a fear of a more terrifying nature." Moonlight fell through the crack of the flysheet of his tent, and as he stared at it he saw a brown blur, and "knew that something lay between himself and the moon." He lay there in frozen immobility until the shadow went away. He now pulled aside the flysheet of the tent. "The night was brilliant. About twenty yards away a great brown creature was swaggering down the hill. He used the word 'swaggering' because the creature had an air of insolent strength about it." His impression was that the creature was about twenty feet high, and was covered with shortish brown hair. It was too erect to be a huge ape; it had a tapering waist and very broad shoulders. Affleck Gray's book contains a photograph of footprints in the snow taken on Ben MacDhui, and they look oddly like the famous photograph of the footprints of the "Abominable Snowman" discovered on the Menlung glacier on Everest by Eric Shipton in 1951.

Frere was inclined to wonder whether the brown-haired creature was real, or whether perhaps it was somehow created by his friend's imagination in that oddly "unreal" state of mind.

In her book *The Secret of Spey*, the writer Wendy Wood describes her own experience on Ben MacDhui. She had reached the entrance to the pass of Lairig Ghru on a snowy day, and was preparing to return when she heard a voice "of gigantic resonance" close behind her. "It seemed to speak with the harsh consonants and full vowels of the Gaelic." She wondered if someone was lying injured in the snow, and tramped around in circles until she was convinced that she was alone. Now feeling afraid, she began to hurry back, and as she descended the mountain, thought she could hear footsteps following her. "She had a strange feeling that something walked immediately behind her." At first she thought it might be echoes of her own footsteps, until she realized that the crunching noises did not exactly correspond with her steps. She asks in her book whether perhaps the strange happenings on Ben MacDhui might be "the concretion of the imaginings of the race, clinging to a particular place, discernible only to those whose racial sensitiveness is open to receive the primal impressions and fears of a bygone day." In other words, she is suggesting that the "ghost" of Ben MacDhui is a "recording".

This seems to be confirmed, to some extent, by an experience recounted by the novelist Joan Grant in her autobiography *Time Out of Mind*. Her book reveals her to be highly psychic. She and her husband were not even on Ben MacDhui but down below near Aviemore; Gray suggests they were on the Lairig Ghru path near Coylum Bridge. For no apparent reason, she was suddenly overwhelmed with fear. "Something – utterly malign, four-legged, and yet obscenely human, invisible and yet solid enough for me to hear the pounding of its hooves, was trying to reach me. If it did I should die for I was far too frightened to know how to defend myself." She fled in terror. "I had run about half a mile when I burst through an invisible barrier behind which I knew I was safe. I knew I was safe now, though a second before I had been in mortal danger; knew it as certainly as though I were a torero who has jumped the barrier in front of a charging bull."

The debate over alien life has two extreme standpoints: those who believe in non-human, sentient beings and those who think such things are just figments of over-active imaginations. Oddly enough, as irreconcilable as these two arguments seem, there is a Far Eastern belief that links the two viewpoints.

Tibetan tradition holds that strong human emotions can create living, semi-corporeal creatures — the *Tulpa*. A *Tulpa* can assume any shape it wishes and may act out its creator's wishes and desires — rather like a European witch's familiar spirit. It is not, however, just an extension of that person's mind. It has an existence of its own and may often outlive its master.

Perhaps the hauntings on Ben MacDhui and all the "alien" beings considered in this book are actually the *real* creations of our super-potent imaginations!

What seems to be emerging from most of these stories about Ben MacDhui is that the chief manifestation is a sudden feeling of depression followed by panic. Joan Grant's account underlines another important point. Tom Lethbridge, who has already been quoted, had observed repeatedly that these sudden unpleasant sensations of fear or "nastiness" seem to have a precisely defined area, so that it is possible to step in or out of them in one single stride. He describes for example how one day he and his wife Mina went to Ladram beach in

Devon to gather seaweed for the garden. At a point on the beach where a small stream flowed from the cliff both experienced an odd feeling of gloom. "I passed into a kind of blanket, or fog, of depression, and, I think, of fear." Mina Lethbridge went off to gather seaweed at the other end of the beach but soon hurried back. "I can't stand this place any longer. There's something frightful here." The following week they returned, on another dull, gray day, and were again greeted by the same feeling of depression – Tom compared it to a bad smell. It was at its worst around the stream, making him feel almost giddy. Mina went to the cliff-top to make a sketch, and had a sudden feeling that she was being urged to jump. Later they verified that someone had committed suicide from this precise spot. Tom noted that it was possible to step in and out of the "depression" – and he noticed it once again when the old lady next door died under strange circumstances after an attempt to practise black magic. An "unpleasant" feeling hung around her house, but it was possible to step in and out of it, as if it was some kind of invisible barrier, like Joan Grant's bullring barrier.

Gray recounts many stories that seem to support Lethbridge's "tape recording" theory. The Scots poet James Hogg, known as the Ettrick Shepherd (because he was a shepherd by profession), once saw a herd of Highland cattle on the far side of the stream, and since they had no right to be there he sent a shepherd to drive them off the land, together with two more farmhands armed with cudgels. But they found no sign of a herd, or even of hoofmarks. No one had seen a herd of cattle in the district that day. It had been some kind of "mirage", or perhaps a "recording" of something long past.

Gray also quotes *The Mountain Vision* by the mountaineer Frank S. Smythe. Smythe describes how, crossing the hills from Morvich to Loch Duich, on a bright sunny day, with a wonderful panorama of cloud-dappled hills and the distant sea, he entered a grassy, sun-warmed defile and "became instantly aware of an aura of evil" in the place. "It was as if something terrible had once happened there, and time had failed to dissipate the atmosphere created by it." On impulse, Smythe decided to eat lunch there. As he smoked his pipe the atmosphere seemed to become increasingly unpleasant. Then, as he strove to be receptive to the strange influence, he seemed to witness a massacre: a score or so of ragged people were straggling wearily through the defile when concealed men rushed down on them with spears and axes, and killed them all. As Smythe hurried on, he seemed to hear screams behind him. He was later able to confirm that a massacre of Highlanders by British troops *had* taken place on the road, but he remained convinced that this is not what he had seen. "The weapons I saw, or seemed to see, were those of an earlier date."

Yet the many strange accounts of invisible presences on Ben MacDhui seem to throw doubt on the notion that the "big gray man" is nothing more than a "recording". George Duncan, an Aberdeen lawyer and a mountaineer, was totally convinced he had seen the devil on the slopes of the mountain. He and a fellow-climber, James A. Parker, had descended from Devil's Point, and were driving in a dog cart along the Derry Road. Duncan said, "All at once, I got the shock of my life by seeing before me a tall figure in a black robe – the conventional figure of the Devil himself – waving his arms, clad in long depending sleeves, coming towards me." He seemed to see the figure surrounded by smoke. In a few moments it passed from view as the cart went round a corner. James A. Parker verified the story. "It was only at dinner that evening he told me that when we were about a mile below Derry Lodge he had looked up to the hillside on his right and seen the Devil about a quarter of a mile away waving his arms to him."

Perhaps the oddest, and in some ways the most interesting, explanation that Gray encountered was given by Captan Sir Hugh Rankin, and his wife. Rankin was a Mahayana Buddhist, and his wife was a Zen Buddhist. He and Lady Rankin were cycling from Rothiemurchus to Mar via the Lairig Ghru pass, and although it was July it was bitterly cold in the pass. At the Pools o' Dee they suddenly felt "the Presence" behind them; they turned and saw a big, olive-complexioned man dressed in a long robe and sandals, with long flowing hair. "We were not in the least afraid. Being Buddhists we at once knew who it was. We at once knelt and made obeisance." They had instantly recognized the stranger as a Bodhisattva, "one of the five 'Perfected Men' who control the destinies of this world, and meet once a year in a cave in the Himalayas". According to Sir Hugh, the Presence addressed them in a language he thought was Sanskrit, and he replied respectfully in Urdu. "All the time the Bodhisattva was with us [he gave the time as about ten minutes] a heavenly host of musicians was playing high up in the sky . . . . Immediately the Bodhisattva left us the music ceased and we never heard it again." It sounds as if they had heard some version of "the Singing". But his comment that the Presence spoke in Sanskrit raises the question of whether Wendy Wood had not mistaken Sanskrit for

Gaelic when she heard it on the mountain.

Shortly before his death, F. W. Holiday, author of a classic book on the Loch Ness monster, advanced the startling theory that the Gray Man, like the Loch Ness monster and the Surrey puma, and possibly the Abominable Snowman of the Himalayas, is a member of "the phantom menagerie", creatures who belong to some other world or dimension. In *The Goblin Universe* he cites various stories about the *Fear Liath More* (the Celtic name for the Gray Man), and goes on:

> Pan, the goat-footed god, is not so funny when you encounter him . . . . The chief symptom of being in the presence of Pan is panic, which the Oxford dictionary defines as "unreasoning and excessive terror, from Greek *panicos*, of god Pan, reputed to cause panic . . . ." The phenomenon is certainly not localised to the Cairngorms. Hamish Corrie, when he was nearing the summit of Sgurr Dearg on Skye, turned back when he was overcome by "an unaccountable panic".

The late John Buchan reported the same effect in the Bavarian Alps. He describes how in 1910 he was returning through a pinewood on a sunny morning with a local forester when panic struck them out of the blue. Both of them fled without speaking until they collapsed from exhaustion on the valley highway below. Buchan comments that a friend of his "ran for dear life" when climbing in Jotunheimen in Norway. The Pan effect may be worldwide.

Holiday connected "the phantom menagerie" (everything from the Loch Ness monster to poltergeist attacks) with alien encounters and Unidentified Flying Objects. Like the psychoanalyst Carl Jung, he suggested that

UFOs and their inhuman passengers are not physical visitors from other planets, but are non-physical "projections". Jung suggested that strange visions and visitations were mass hallucinations projected by the human "mass subconscious", but Ted Holiday theorized that the intruders might be non-physical intelligences from a "neighboring dimension". This "goblin universe" of his book's title, is peopled by creatures that can invade and, to a certain extent, affect our physical world; their reasons for doing so seem to range from the saintly to the demonic. If the reader is inclined to reject Holiday's theory as pure science fiction, they should first remember that almost every religion on Earth suggests a similar "ethereal world" attached to our own and that quantum physicists have long considered "parallel universes" to be not only possible, but likely.

Affleck Gray is also willing to consider the "space visitors" theory as an explanation of the Ben MacDhui phenomena. He points out that in 1954 an ex-taxi driver named George King inaugurated the Aetherius Society in Caxton Hall, London. King claimed that he had met the Master Jesus on Holdstone Down, North Devon, and been made aware that he had been chosen as the primary mental channel of certain Space Intelligences. He was told to travel the world, his task being to serve as the channel for "charging" eighteen mountains with cosmic energy. One of these mountains was Creag an Leth-Choin, three miles north-west of Ben MacDhui, and King asserts that there is a huge dome-shaped auditorium, a retreat of the Great White Brotherhood, in the bowels of Ben MacDhui. Another group of "seekers", the Active Truth Academy in Edinburgh, also believe that Ben MacDhui "has become the earth-fall for

Sir Laurens van der Post

space beings". But it is clear from Gray's chapter on Space Beings that he regards this explanation with skepticism.

If we wish for a "scientific" explanation of the Ben MacDhui phenomena, then the likeliest seems to be that the answer lies in Ben MacDhui itself: that the "panic" is caused by some natural phenomenon, a kind of "earth force" which may be connected with the earth's magnetic field. There are areas of the earth's surface where birds lose their way because the lines of earth magnetism somehow cancel one another out, forming a magnetic vortex. "Ley-hunters" also believe that so-called "ley lines" – which connect sacred sites such as churches, barrows and standing stones – are basically lines of magnetic force. Many are also convinced that places in which this force is exceptionally powerful are likely to be connected with "supernatural" occurrences – in fact, that such places "record" human emotions, producing the effects that are described as "hauntings". This explanation would account for Frank Smythe's experience of the "haunted" valley where the massacre had occurred.

The non-scientific explanation may be sought in the belief of most primitive peoples that the earth is alive, that certain places are holy, and that such places are inhabited by spirits. The Western mind is inclined to dismiss such beliefs as superstition; but many travellers who have been in close contact with them are inclined to be more open-minded. In *The Lost World of the Kalahari*, Laurens van der Post tells how, when he was seeking the vanished Bushmen of South Africa, his guide Samutchoso took him to a place called the Slippery Hills. The guide insisted that there must be no hunting as they approached the hills, or the gods would be angry. Van der Post forgot to tell his advance party, and they shot a warthog. From then on they ran into an endless stream of bad luck. When Samutchoso tried to pray, van der Post saw that he was pulled over backward by some unknown force. All their technical equipment began to malfunction. Then Samutchoso "consulted" the spirits and began to speak to invisible presences. He told van der Post that they *were* angry, and would have killed him if he had tried to pray again. Van der Post suggested that they should all write a message of apology, and that this should be buried in a bottle at the foot of a sacred rock. Apparently this worked; the spirits were propitiated, and suddenly the equipment ceased to malfunction. Through the guide, the "spirits" told van der Post that he would find bad news waiting for him when he reached the next place on his route. In fact his assistant found a message saying that his father had died and he had to return home immediately. After all this, van der Post had no doubt of the real existence of the "earth spirits" worshipped by primitive people.

F. W. Holiday's view was that the explanation of such phenomena as the "Gray Man" lay somewhere between these two sets of explanations: the scientific and the "supernatural". But he believed that the Western mind will be capable of grasping the answer only when it has broadened its conception of science.

4

The Devil's Footprints

It is not surprising that some of those who have encountered malign forces on Ben MacDhui believed that they were attacked by the Devil. In some ways Old Nick may be considered the original "alien invader"; the archetype of inhuman evil bent on our destruction. Whether or not one believes in Satan, it is hard not to be given pause by evidence of a goat-footed biped stalking through the Devon snows in 1855.

Was it an alien, a demon or some unidentified natural phenomena? In this chapter readers must decide for themselves.

The winter of 1855 was an exceptionally severe one, even in the south-west of England, where winters are usually mild. On the morning of February 8, Albert Brailsford, the principal of the village school in Topsham, Devon, walked out of his front door to find that it had snowed in the night. And he was intrigued to notice a line of footprints – or rather hoofprints – that ran down the village street. At first glance they looked like the ordinary hoofprints of a shod horse; but a closer look showed that this was impossible, for the prints ran in a continuous line, one in front of the other. If it was a horse, then it must have had only one leg, and hopped along the street. And if the unknown creature had two legs, then it must have placed one carefully in front of the other, as if walking along a tightrope. What was odder still was that the prints – each about four inches long – were only about eight inches apart. And each print was very clear, as if it had been branded into the frozen snow with a hot iron.

The villagers of Topsham were soon following the track southward through the snow. And they halted in astonishment when the hoofprints came to a halt at a brick wall. They were more baffled than ever when someone discovered that they continued on the other side of the wall, and that the snow on top of the wall was undisturbed. The tracks approached a haystack, and continued on the other side of it, although the hay showed no sign that a heavy creature had clambered over it. The prints passed under gooseberry bushes, and were even seen on rooftops. It began to look as if some insane practical joker had decided to set the village an insoluble puzzle.

But it was soon clear that this explanation was also out of the question. Excited investigators tracked the prints for mile after mile over the Devon countryside. They seemed to wander erratically through a number of small towns and villages – Lympstone, Exmouth, Teignmouth, Dawlish, as far as Totnes, about halfway to Plymouth. If it was a practical joker, he would have had to cover forty miles, much of it through deep snow. Moreover, such a joker would surely have hurried forward to cover the greatest distance possible; in fact, the steps often approached front doors, then changed their mind and went away again. At some point the creature had crossed the estuary of the river Exe – it looked as if the crossing was between Lympstone and Powderham. Yet there were also footprints in Exmouth, farther south, as if it had turned back on its tracks. There was no logic in its meandering course.

Those who believe that the US Government is involved in a cover-up of human-alien contact were amazed by the disclosure of the Robertson Report — a CIA funded investigation that directly advocated the suppression of UFO reports and independent UFO investigation.

This panel of scientists, chaired by Dr H. P. Robertson, considered various well-authenticated UFO sightings for five days in January 1953, but their conclusions were not declassified until 1975. Among their suggestions for the federal authorities to consider were the covert surveillance and infiltration of UFO enthusiast groups, a deliberate policy of squashing, debunking or officially ignoring UFO sightings, and a major anti-UFO propaganda campaign. For the latter, scientists suggested employing the skills of expert "psychologists familiar with mass psychology," and the filmmakers at Walt Disney Studios.

This document might have caused much more of a public stir when it was discovered, if it had not been for one thing — the scientists advocated these extreme (and possibly unconstitutional) measures because they had concluded that *all* UFO reports were either fraudulent or mistaken. As far as the Robertson Panel was concerned there were no alien invaders, but public musing on such matters constituted "a threat to the orderly functioning of the protective organs of the body politic."

In places it looked as if the "horseshoe" had a split in it, suggesting a cloven hoof. It was the middle of the Victorian era, and few country people doubted the existence of the Devil. Men armed with guns and pitchforks followed the trail; when night came people locked their doors and kept loaded shotguns at hand.

It was another week before the story reached the newspapers; on February 16, 1855 *The Times* told the story, adding that most gardens in Lympstone showed some trace of the strange visitor. The following day the *Plymouth Gazette* carried a report, and mentioned the theory of a clergyman that the creature could have been a kangaroo – apparently unaware that a kangaroo has claws. A report in the Exeter *Flying Post* made the slightly more plausible suggestion that it was a bird. But a correspondent in the *Illustrated London News* dismissed this idea, pointing out that no bird leaves a horse-shoe-shaped print. He added that he had passed a five-month winter in the backwoods of Canada, and had never seen a more clearly defined track.

In the *Illustrated London News* for March 3, the great naturalist and anatomist Richard Owen announced dogmatically that the footmarks were those of the hind foot of a badger, and suggested that many badgers had come out of hibernation that night to seek food. He did not explain why all these badgers hopped along on one hind foot. (Five years later, he was to be equally dogmatic – and equally wrong – on the subject of Charles Darwin and the origin of species.) Another correspondent, a doctor, described how he and another doctor "bestowed considerable time in endeavoring to discover the peculiarities of this most singular impression" (the Victorians loved this kind of pompous language). He claimed that "on more minute examination of the tracks, we could distinctly see the impressions of the toes and pad of the foot of an animal." His own candidate was an otter. Another correspondent, who signed himself "Ornither", was quite certain that they were the prints of a Great Bustard, whose outer toes, he claimed, were rounded. Another gentleman, from Sudbury, said he had recently seen impressions of rats surrounding a potato patch, and that they looked exactly like the drawings of "the devil's footprints". He thought that the rats had been leaping through the snow, landing with their full body weight and producing a roughly horseshoe-shaped impression. A Scottish correspondent thought that the culprit could be a hare or polecat bounding through the snow. These suggestions are less absurd than they sound. They would certainly explain the most baffling feature of the footprints – that they followed one upon another, as if made by a one-legged animal. But they still fail to explain why they continued for forty miles or so!

Perhaps the likeliest hypothesis is one put forward by Geoffrey Household, who edited a small book containing all the major correspondence on the matter. He comments as follows, in a letter to the author:

> I think that Devonport dockyard released, by accident, some sort of experimental balloon. It broke free from its moorings, and trailed two shackles on the end of ropes. The impression left in the snow by these shackles went up the sides of houses, over haystacks, etc . . . . A Major Carter, a local man, tells me that his grandfather worked at Devonport at the time, and that the whole thing was hushed up because the balloon destroyed a number of conservatories, greenhouses, windows, etc. He says that the balloon finally came down at Honiton.

This information is fascinating, and could well represent the solution of the mystery. But if so there is still one major anomaly to be explained. A glance at the map of the "footprints" will show that they meandered in a kind of circle between Topsham and Exmouth. Would

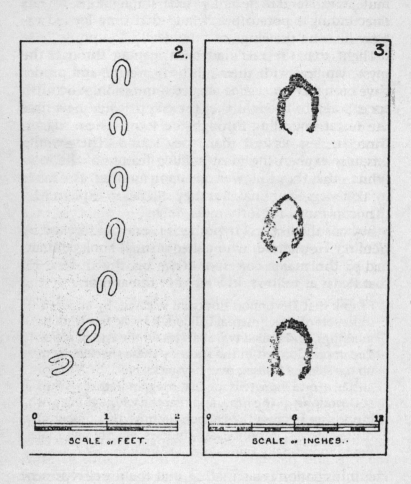

Two eye-witness sketches of the "Devil's Hoofprints", 1855

an escaped balloon drift around so erratically? Surely its route would tend to be a more or less straight line, in the direction of the prevailing wind which, moreover, was blowing from the east.

The fact that it took a week for the first report of the mystery to appear in print means that certain vital clues have been lost for ever. It would be interesting to know, for example, whether the snow that fell that night was the first snow of February 1855. It had been a hard winter that year, and many small animals, including rats, rabbits and badgers, must have been half starved by February and have been out looking for food. The letter to the *Plymouth Gazette* (dated February 17) begins: "Thursday night, the 8th of February, was marked by a heavy fall of snow, followed by rain and boisterous wind from the east, and in the morning frost". Small animals had probably been out every night, but it was not until that Friday morning, with its fresh carpet of snow, that their tracks were noticed for the first time. Such tracks would have sunk deep into the soft snow, and would have been further deepened by the rain before they were frozen solid. This would explain why they seemed to be "branded" into the snow.

But if the ground was already covered with snow before the night of February 8, then one more plausible theory would have to be abandoned. And in any case it fails to explain how the tracks managed to wander over rooftops and haystacks . . . . At this distance in time, the only certainty seems to be that the mystery is now insoluble.

5

Alien Horrors – Goatsuckers, Cattle Mutilations and the West Virginia Mothman

One skeptic has suggested that if extraterrestrials were as benevolent and intelligent as some UFO enthusiasts believe, they would have landed on the White House lawn years ago, instead of choosing some godforsaken spot in the middle of nowhere, tormenting, humiliating and occasionally sexually abusing some unfortunate farm laborer, then taking off without leaving so much as a greetings card or a cure for cancer. Even allowing for alien indifference to human social mores, this sort of behavior sounds like bad manners.

The lack of physical evidence for alien life is the skeptic's strongest argument against its existence. Yet, there is well-authenticated evidence from around the world that points to considerable non-human activity. The problem is that if crop circles, abductions and cattle mutilations are the handiwork of alien visitors, they suggest creatures with a bizarre and sometimes sadistic sense of humour. At best, the aliens seem to regard us with the same detachment we feel towards laboratory rats.

Goatsuckers

The killing began during March 1995, in the mountainous, inland districts of Morovis and Orocovis on the

75

Caribbean island of Puerto Rico. Each morning, unlucky inhabitants would find their smaller livestock (such as chickens, sheep and goats) lying dead in their pens, drained of blood from a single deep puncture wound to the neck or chest. Within weeks, the slaughter had spread across the whole island, reaching near-epidemic proportions. While the authorities tried to ignore the problem, the general populace became increasingly frightened. How long could it be before the vampire turned on human beings?

By Caribbean standards, Puerto Rico is relatively well-off, with stable industries and a good tourist trade, as well as enjoying favored trading status with the USA. Nevertheless, the loss of valuable livestock hits their owner hard, so the victims soon became the hunters. Up to 200-man search parties made nightly patrols, and animals were carefully guarded. Yet it was not until six months had passed that the Chupacabras (a Spanish word meaning "goat-sucker") was actually seen in the flesh.

In September 1995, housewife Madelyne Tolentino spotted the monster near the town of Canivanas in the east of the island. She described a fanged, furry "kangaroo-like" beast with bulging red eyes. After this first appearance, the Chupacabras was sighted regularly during the next four months. Later reports suggested a pig or humanoid-headed creature with a tail and spikes – or pointed growths of hair – running down its back. It walked erect, stood about four-feet high and had clawed hands. Some witnesses also reported wings. In November, local ufologist Jorges Martin collated the sightings and posted a sketch of the Goatsucker on the Internet.

By mid-December 1995, over a thousand animals were

estimated to have been killed by the Chupacabras, including goats, chickens, turkeys, sheep, rabbits, cats, dogs and even cows and horses. Fortunately, the creature seemed to have no taste for human blood, although in November a red-eyed, hairy beast was seen to break open a bedroom window, reach in and tear a teddy bear to pieces – presumably out of frustration. Then, in early January 1996, the attacks dwindled and stopped.

Theories as to what the killer might have been were, of course, running wild. The government insisted that the attacks were the work of dogs or feral monkeys. This explanation cut little ice with eye-witnesses, since dogs and monkeys are not known to be bloodsuckers, or to leave gluey slime on their victims (another typical Goatsucker characteristic.)

The odor of the monster led to another line of speculation altogether – the Chupacabras was said to stink of sulphur. In a devoutly Catholic country, five years from the second Millennium, the whiff of brimstone was bound to raise fears of demonic intervention. Many believed the time of pestilence and the rule of the Antichrist, foretold in the Book of Revelations, was at hand.

The secret testing of genetically designed weapons by the US Government was another favorite theory among the islanders. This may not be as unjustified a slur as might first be imagined. Since the passing of the Freedom of Information Act in 1981, the United States military have been forced to admit to testing various "defence projects" – including radiation, biological weapons and mind-changing drugs, both on their own population and those of friendly nations. More specifically, a team of American doctors from the Rockefeller

Institute induced cancer in an unrecorded number of Puerto Ricans in 1931 – at least thirteen are known to have died as a direct result. The team leader, Cornelius Rhoades, gave the following, measured explanation when the project's activities became public: "The Porto [sic] Ricans are the dirtiest, laziest, most degenerate, thievish race of men ever inhabiting this sphere . . . . I have done my best to further the process of extermination by killing off eight and transplanting cancer into several more . . . ." The US Government punished Rhoades by putting him in charge of two major chemical weapon projects in the 1940s, giving him a seat on the Atomic Energy Commission and awarding him the Legion of Merit. Why indeed should Puerto Ricans trust Uncle Sam?

The island's reputation as a major region for UFO sightings led to predictable extraterrestrial speculations. The most imaginative of these suggested that ET's were attempting to undermine the human race through the spread of HIV and other blood infections. This ignored the fact that only one attack on a human had been reported – in that case the creature had seized forty-four-year-old Osvaldo Rosando, but had not bitten him. But the ET lobby argued that the Goatsucker's sudden appearance suggested that it was not native to Puerto Rico, and that its origin was as likely to be outer space as anywhere else.

There were, however, a few matters on which everyone, except the government, agreed. The Goatsucker was physically powerful; it seemed to have little difficulty ripping open metal cages or, in one case, tearing down a 16 by 14 foot galvanised iron gate. It also had to be stealthy and cunning – perhaps even intelligent – to evade all efforts to capture and kill it. Moreover, few of the island's inhabitants believed they had heard the last of it. Some suggested that it had slunk back into the forested, mountainous territory of the interior, with its extensive cave system, to hibernate for the winter. In fact, the vampire struck again when Spring returned in March 1966. Farmer Arturo Rodriguez awoke to find thirty of his hens and fighting cocks slaughtered. Each had deep puncture marks on the neck or chest, and all had been drained of blood. It looked as if the Chupa-cabras had returned with a burning thirst.

Ufologist Jorges Martin's internet reports and Puerto Rican media coverage of the vampire had by now caused intense interest abroad, especially in the Gulf of Mexico countries, and the southern United States. At about the same time the Goatsucker was making its 1996 come-back, the popular Miami-based talkshow "Cristina", hosted by Cristina Saralege, started to feature regular updates on Chupacabras attacks. The newspapers loved the story ("GOATSUCKER STRIKES AGAIN!!!" is cer-tainly the tabloid editor's dream of a front-page head-line) and soon the Chupacabras was a household word. Goatsucker t-shirts – a certain index of fame – were rushed into the shops, and comedians and newspaper cartoonists seized gratefully on the new material. And the Chupacabras responded to celebrity by moving to the mainland.

During March 1996, over sixty animal deaths (includ-ing goats, chickens, ducks and geese) in the Hispanic neighborhood of South Miami had been blamed on the Goatsucker. One woman claimed to have seen "a dog-like figure standing up with two short hands in the air." But zoologist Ron Magill insisted that the marks on the victims were "classic canine punctures from dogs." Investigating Detective Pat Brickman snapped scornfully that the witnesses were "idiots who believe everything they see on TV."

By late April, farmers in the Sinlaoa, Jalisco, Veracruz and eight other states of Mexico had reported dozens of bloodsucking attacks – mostly on goats. Many locals refused to send their children out to school, and farmers were afraid to work after sunset. In these poverty stricken areas, often entirely dependent on livestock for survival, the attacks were a real social and economic disaster. Officials admitted that the animal casualties were genuine, but placed the blame on coyotes and bats driven to desperation by the recent drought. No one explained why such attacks had never happened before in a country particularly prone to droughts.

Then came the most ominous development so far - reports of attacks on people. In April, twenty-year-old Juana Tizoc appeared on Mexico's major news network, "Televisa", displaying bite-like lacerations on her neck. She claimed to have been attacked by a "winged creature". Many others now came forward claiming to have been bitten by the Goatsucker. Skeptics noted that none of these attacks were fatal, or even serious, and alleged self-mutilation for the purpose of self-aggrandisement.

Non-violent Goatsucker confrontations were also reported. In the state of Nayarit, Mexican police spotted a red-eyed creature that snarled at them before leaping a six-foot fence. In Arizona, in May, the Ezspinoza family were terrorized in their home by an animal that "mumbled and gestured and smelt like a wet dog." In the same month in Zapotal, Mexico, Violeta Colorado's dogs managed to corner a strange, weirdly hissing animal, which got away. That night, nine sheep were killed in a nearby pasture, their throats punctured and their blood drained.

On July 8, 1947, Lieutenant Walter Haut – a Public Information Officer for the US Army Air Corps – issued what was possibly the most important press release in human history. He announced that the Roswell Army Airfield in New Mexico had found and recovered a crashed "flying disc." A radio station in Albuquerque picked up and ran the story immediately, but while the news was still being broadcast a wire came through from the FBI: "Attention Albuquerque: Cease Transmission. Repeat. Cease Transmission. National Security Item. Do Not Transmit. Stand By . . . ."

The following day, the army issued a statement saying that Haut's UFO report was "a mistake" – the object being held was actually a smashed weather balloon. Although some reporters noted that a suspiciously large amount of official muscle went into silencing the flying saucer story, most took the military's word on trust.

The Roswell incident then lay, all but forgotten, until 1978, when nuclear physicist Stanton Freidman decided to research the case further. He interviewed 62 people, military and civilian, who all claimed different degrees of involvement with the "flying disc" recovery. The resulting story has, much to the annoyance of the US military, thoroughly engaged the public's imagination . . . .

On the stormy night of July 2, 1947, *two* UFO's were said to have crashed at Corona, near Roswell. Five "aliens" – small humanoids with domed skulls, almond-shaped eyes and slits for mouth and nose – were recovered with the craft. Four were dead, but one was said to be still alive. Autopsies were performed on the corpses at Roswell, but the UFO wreckage was removed to the Wright-Patterson Air Force Base at Dayton, Ohio. Lieutenant Haut was told to issue the press statement by the base commander, Colonel Blanchard, shortly before Commanding General Roger Ramsey issued a total information clampdown.

The US military have continued to deny the Roswell-UFO reports, but in 1994 they were forced to make an uncomfortable admission. The US General Accounting Office (GAO) had just announced its intention to review the available Roswell documents, when the Air Force rushed out its own 25-page report in which they admitted that the weather balloon story had been a lie. The "craft," they said, had actually been a top-secret balloon devised to listen for Soviet nuclear tests.

This new story has failed to end the speculation over the Roswell incident and, in fact, has only served to prove that there *was* a cover-up over the events in New Mexico on July 2, 1947. Witnesses of the recovered debris, including Walter Haut, continue to insist that what they saw was *not* a balloon of any sort. Whether or not aliens crashed at Corona, few Ufologists are now willing to take the Air Force's word on trust alone.

At the time of this writing (January 1997), authenticated "vampiristic" attacks on animals have also been reported in Costa Rica, El Salvador, Guatemala and as far south as Brazil and Amazonia. In October 1996, the Goatsucker even managed to cross the Atlantic, attacking a herd of twenty-eight sheep in Idanha-a-Novo in

Portugal. The farmer claimed that each animal had suffered a single deep puncture to the left side of the neck – nine died.

Even taking into account the inevitable hoaxes and misdiagnosed fatalities, it is impossible to argue away the basic fact that something or someone has been killing animals on a large scale. Yet no one seems any closer to suggesting to what species the Chupacabras might belong. Zoologists find the idea of a large, winged vampire on two legs ridiculous, yet their own explanations have been unconvincing. One suggestion has been that a previously unknown breed of giant vampire bat (with a five-foot wingspan and weighing 20 lbs), was driven north by the destruction of the South American rainforests. But no one has explained why it was not sighted sooner, and why it flew many thousands of miles to Puerto Rico before it first stopped for a meal of chicken blood.

The correlation between media coverage and the spread of Goatsucker incidents raises one disturbing possibility. The ritual slaughter of animals has been common throughout history, and is still a widespread religious practice today. Commenting on the Chupacabras single puncture wound phenomenon, Marielena Hoyo, director of Mexico City's Chapultepec Zoo, noted a reference in the Old Testament Book of Leviticus to a perforating tool designed to spill animal blood for ritual purposes. She went on to comment that zoo security was being tightened "in case anyone wants to make-believe they're the Chupacabras."

In recent years, sadistic attacks on animals have become more frequent in Europe and North America. "Horse-rippers" have been recorded in Europe for centuries, but never at the level reached in the 1980s and 90s, when horrific reports of mutilated and disembowelled horses became commonplace. The sexual nature of these attacks is suggested by the fact that the animal's genitals are often a target for particular mutilation. When arrests and convictions have been made, the perpetrators invariably prove to be lone males suffering from psycho-sexual disorders.

Cattle Mutilations

North America has been experiencing its own version of the Goatsucker epidemic since 1967, the date of the first recorded "cattle-mutilations". On the evening of Friday, September 8, 1967, a three year-old Appaloosa named Lady, failed to make her customary return to the corral where her mother Snippy grazed. Harry King, who ranched in the San Luis Valley of southern Colorado found her lying on her side in a clearing, the flesh stripped from her head and neck. The rest of the body was untouched. The skinning had been performed with remarkable skill. Harry's brother-in-law Berle thought he smelt a "medicated smell" around the dead horse.

Newspaper reports were inclined to link the mutilation with mysterious lights in the sky and large flying objects that had been seen over the San Luis Valley – Harry King's eighty-seven-year-old mother had seen a "large object" flying over the ranch house on the night Lady disappeared.

But it was not until three years later, in 1970, that cattle mutilation became an epidemic. In her book *An Alien Harvest*, Linda Moulton Howe reports that "between 1970 and 1974, twenty-two mutilated carcasses had been reported in Minnesota," while dozens of others were reported from Wisconsin, South Dakota, Iowa, Kansas and Nebraska. Most of these were cows, found dead and hideously mutilated in the Midwest pastures. Damage varied from victim to victim, but there were common links. Most of the butchered cattle had black, or mostly black hides, raising fears of Satanic cults. The animals were killed singly, never in groups as with the Goatsucker. The ears were usually removed, as were the udders, sex organs and anus – these latter being "cored-out" from the body as if by a specially designed instrument. Sometimes, as with the Chupacabras attacks, the victim's blood had been drained. No footprints could be found, and there was no other piece of significant forensic evidence. It was as if the butcher had dropped down from the sky, killed, drained and mutilated the animal, and then had left the way it came . . . .

In *An Alien Harvest*, Linda Moulton Howe explains how she came to conclude that "extraterrestrials" may be responsible for the mutilations. She heard of a woman called Judy Dorati, who in May 1973 was driving back from a bingo game in Houston, Texas, with her teenage daughter Cindy and other relatives when they saw a bright light in the sky. They stopped to watch it more closely – then she remembers no more until she found herself getting back into the car, "thirsty and nauseous." After a period of headaches and nightmares, she underwent hypnosis, and recalled how she and her daughter had both been taken aboard a UFO and subjected to physical examination. But they had also seen a calf "levitated" in a beam of light and taken on board. She saw this cow subjected to "surgery" that seemed to involve a kind of laser, and which excised tissues from the living (but apparently stupefied) animal. The calf was then lowered back, dead, to the pasture.

What is happening, according to Judy Dorati, is that the extraterrestrials are engaged in some kind of operation that involves testing the soil, water, vegetation and animal life. She was afraid that her daughter Cindy – who was unconscious on a table – might be subjected to the same kind of excisions; but apparently – she learned from the "beings" – this was not part of the intention. Human beings are studied, but not harmed.

At the peak of the cattle mutilations, in 1976, at least twenty-three states were affected. In his book *Messengers of Deception*, Jacques Vallee noted that "In an eighteen-month period before January 1977 there were 700 mutilations in 15 western states. More than 180 cases occurred in Colorado alone in 1975." Eyes, as well as ears were often missing. The teeth, tongue and the flesh of the lower jaw were sometimes removed. At other times, as in the case of Lady, all the flesh from the head and neck might be missing, but in many such cases, internal organs such as the brain or heart, were also removed. It seems unlikely that the perpetrator ate the flesh, for the lean meat was left virtually untouched, while the offal was either taken away or "arranged" on or around the corpse (in the manner of London's Victorian killer of prostitutes, Jack the Ripper.) Pieces of hide were expertly stripped, leaving the flesh underneath undamaged, but were taken from such odd areas and in such odd shapes that they could not possibly have been put to any subsequent practical use. Sometimes the result was almost artistic – perfect circles and squares, reminiscent of Britain's crop-circles in the 1980s and 90s, would be removed. There were also special, bizarre touches: Sheriff George Yarnell of Elbert County, Colorado, reported finding a mutilated cow with a strangely bulging udder. Veterinary examination revealed that everything but the organ's skin had been removed and replaced with sand.

Investigations brought to light interesting, but unenlightening, facts. The mutilation incisions, for example, were of surgical precision. Broken bones often suggested that the bodies had been dropped from a height, fuelling speculation among Ufologists that the animals had been carried aloft into a flying saucer, then thrown out. This would also explain the lack of footprints and blood at the scene. Needle-jabs were found in major arteries and traces of tranquillising chemicals such as nicotine sulphate and PCP (which drug-users call "angel dust".)

Newspapers were inclined to blame hippies and/or Satanic cults for the atrocities. After the Manson murders of the late 1960s, including the butchery of the pregnant Sharon Tate, the American public believed the hippies were capable of anything. Conspiracy buffs had an even more sinister explanation – that the government was conducting tests with experimental secret weapons. The objection to the hippie/satanist theory was that such groups do not usually have access to high-tech equipment, and that in any case, they would instantly arouse attention out in the farmlands of the mid-west. The conspiracy theory founders on the fact that the US Army can certainly afford their own heifers. Another theory – that the mutilations were intended to terrify the public – was easily disproved by the fact that the public at large was indifferent to the killings, and probably did not believe in them anyway. The only people who were terrified were the farmers and their accountants.

In 1980, former FBI agent Kenneth Rommel published a deflationary study of the phenomena, concluding that the cattle deaths were all from natural causes – echoing a report from Kansas University that the cause of death was the bacterial disease blackleg – and that the "mutilations" were caused by predators. The only extraordinary aspect of the whole business, he remarked irritably, was the mass hysteria aroused by these events. The media seem to have taken the implied criticism to heart, and have since given cattle mutilation stories little or no coverage.

Others were less inclined to drop the subject. These include the farmers who continue to lose cattle (although, fortunately, at a much reduced rate than during the 1970s) and investigators who noted the various issues evaded in Rommel's report. They pointed out that Rommel failed to explain the complete lack of blood in so many of the dead cattle – such a level of vampirism is unknown among scavengers. In fact, it should be medically impossible – when a certain amount of blood is drawn from a corpse, the arteries collapse through loss of internal pressure, blocking the further release of fluid. In the case of mutilated cattle (and "Goatsucker" victims) examiners find the body to be quite empty. The scavenger theory is also implausible. Autopsies on mutilated cattle often speak of surgically precise dissection, which looks totally unlike marks caused by the teeth of what mid-western farmers call "varmints". The neck and skull of Lady, the first recorded victim, had been cleanly stripped of flesh, and were completely white. (Anyone who has seen bones in a butcher's shop will know they are red). Some autopsies have noted that the flesh seems to have been cut with something very hot – such as a laser beam. Moreover, some incisions were not cuts in the strict sense of the term. A knife or scalpel damages the cell-structure when it cuts, yet in some mutilation cases the cells of the wounds were found to have simply separated from each other, like the Red Sea in the Bible.

Inevitably, the UFO theory was by far the most popular explanation. During the cattle mutilation peak of the 1970s, especially in the American Midwest, there were thousands of sightings of unidentified flying objects. In 1973, the police in Dayton, Ohio received reports of over eighty UFO sightings in their area alone. One was from a woman who claimed to have actually seen a flying saucer land and kill two cows. Unmarked helicopters observed hovering near subsequent mutilation sites and the intimidation of witnesses by black-suited "officials" (nicknamed Men-in-Black, or MIBs) led conspiracy theorists to suggest that the US government had signed a "secret treaty" with some alien power, which in turn raised the question of the terms of the agreement, and what kind of franchise the government has allowed the aliens.

Some abductees who have recovered memories of "missing time" through hypnotherapy (see chapter 6) have expressed the opinion that, with a certain amount of "official permission", the extraterrestrials are engaged in a study of life on Earth, and that cattle mutilation is just one aspect of this project. Some writers have pointed out that extraterrestrial science is bound to be incomprehensible to human minds since we do not know their methods or long-term purpose.

The capriciousness of many UFO-related phenomena struck American writer, John A. Keel, while he was investigating the paranormal goings-on around the town of Point Pleasant, West Virginia in 1967 (the year of the "Lady" killing). For months the area had suffered a spate of cattle mutilations and UFO sightings. These latter were so common the locals had almost come to take strange lights in the sky for granted. People in the area of the Camp Conley Road complained that UFOs buzzed them every night from 8.30 p.m. onward. "You can set your watch by 'em," resident James Lilly told a group of startled reporters as brilliant lights glided across the sky above them. Many people travelled hundreds of miles to see the light-show, and the otherwise unremarkable Camp Conley Road became a busy tourist resort by night. Cows and pigs were the main victims of the mutilations, but dogs and cats were also killed and dissected. The blood was drained, but there was no sign of it around the dead animal, organs and hide had been removed, and the perpetrator's footprints could not be detected, even on muddy or snow-covered ground.

The Mothman

On top of all this, there were reports of the "Mothman". Many independent witnesses reported seeing this freakish, humanoid figure, taller than a man, with no discernible head, yet with two large, glowing red eyes in the chest area. The nickname "Mothman" came from the short, dark fur that covered its body like a furry moth, and its huge wings. "Mothman" lurked by the road in isolated areas, appeared in people's gardens or, occasionally, would chase the cars of terrified witnesses, floating alongside them. Those who reported this stressed that it seemed to be levitating rather than flying, since its wings were not seen to flap. Although many people suspected a connection between "Mothman" and the other bizarre events in the Point Pleasant area, nobody actually claimed to have seen "Mothman" descend from a UFO or attack a cow.

Many witnesses later claimed that they had been subsequently interviewed by "men in black" who claimed to be from some government agency. As usual in such cases, all attempts to link the "MIBs" to government agencies were a failure. In fact, some witnesses were inclined to doubt whether the MIBs were *human*. Their skins were a strange olive colour, their tone of voice was oddly mechanical, and their use of the language was tentative and unpractised, as if newly-learned. Many of the questions they asked were ridiculously inconsequential – in fact, they seemed less like FBI agents than escaped mental patients. Interviewees often reported that these eccentrics arrived and left during the hours of darkness in old-fashioned cars with the headlights turned off. One MIB was even reported to have tried to drink a bowl of Jello, as if he had never seen the dessert before and thought it to be a liquid.

Throughout 1967, Keel and other UFO investigators came under increasing harassment by unknown persons who seemed determined to discourage them or drive them to paranoia. Their phones were tapped, mail went missing and their movements were tracked with uncanny accuracy. Keel tells of driving up to a West Virginian farm on the spur of the moment to ask if they had seen anything odd. The farmer was first hostile, but when Keel persuaded a local journalist to reassure him, he explained that he had received a warning telephone call about a dangerous lunatic called John Keel, who was going to call on him. The caller claimed to be, and sounded like, the farmer's neighbor – who had, in fact, been working in the fields all day, miles from any telephone. Even stranger, the warning was sent over an hour before Keel made the snap decision to turn into the farm's entrance or even to drive to that area. If the MIBs were robots, they were apparently precognitive robots. Harassment of investigators increased over the months and included threatening phone calls, fake messages and tremendous bills for out-going calls that were never made (it should be remembered that 1960s non-computerised telephone exchanges could be easily manipulated by anyone skilled in electronics – so it is unnecessary to postulate that the phone company was involved in the conspiracy).

One day, a young woman rang and told Keel that someone called "Apol" had a message for him. She said that this Man-in-Black lookalike admitted to being an alien and claimed to know of future events. When the girl was under hypnosis, "Apol" spoke through her mouth; later, he began to speak with Keel direct over the telephone. In these conversations, "Apol" accurately predicted a number of plane crashes and other events, but was not totally reliable. For example, he warned that Pope Paul VI would be stabbed at Istanbul airport during a visit to Turkey. Nothing happened, but three years later a man with a knife tried and failed to kill the Pope at Manila airport. "Apol" also predicted that Martin Luther King would be shot through the throat in Memphis on February 4, 1968. In fact the killing took place on April 4, but the other details were correct.

Keel felt that he was in an impossible position. How

could he warn people of forthcoming dangers on such unreliable evidence? Yet he had to admit that "Apol" was usually correct. The alien apologized for his inaccuracies, explaining that he was naturally "outside" time and space and found the transition confusing. One warning, however, he was insistent upon – there would be a massive power failure affecting most of the United States on December 15, 1967. It would happen the moment President Lyndon Johnson turned on the fairy lights on the giant White House Christmas tree (a televized event in the United States). Keel watched the ceremony and was relieved when no power failure occurred. At that point, the broadcast was interrupted by a newsflash – the Silver Bridge, spanning the Ohio River at Point Pleasant had collapsed killing dozens of motorists (thirty-eight are known to have died, but some "missing persons" are also believed drowned in the disaster).

Keel was horrified – and furious. He felt that "Apol" had deliberately misinformed him about the one disaster they could have averted – his contacts in UFO-haunted Point Pleasant might have accepted a warning, even from such a weird source. If the bridge had been checked the stress damage that threatened its collapse might have be recognized. It appeared that "Apol" had wanted the catastrophe to happen; no amount of "disorientation" could have explained his downright misleading warning.

As if the Silver Bridge disaster had eased some psychic tension, or brought a chain of events to its climax, the bizarre incidents that had plagued Point Pleasant suddenly diminished in 1968. But seven years later, when Keel published his account in *The Mothman Prophecies* (1975) there were still sporadic outbreaks, leading him to describe West Virginia as a "paranormal hotzone."

Keel notes in the book that West Virginia has always had a reputation for strange occurrences. Native Americans had long settled the whole eastern seaboard by the time the first Europeans arrived but, in spite of their rivalry for land, none lived in West Virginia. The settlers had wiped out all the neighboring tribes before anyone thought to ask why, so we shall now probably never know.

The Holy Grail of Ufology is, of course, provable alien contact – alive or dead. In early 1995, just such evidence seemed to have been unearthed. A British businessman called Ray Santilli, claimed to have obtained film showing one of the Roswell "aliens," undergoing an autopsy at the hands of military surgeons.

The rights to show the twenty-minute, silent, black-and-white film were quickly sold to the Fox network and, that August, it was screened amid the sort of hype usually reserved for a blockbuster movie. The film itself shows a child-sized body with the domed head, bulging eyes and tiny nose – apparently one of the so-called "Grays," familiar to anyone who has read Whitley Strieber's *Communion*, or seen the movie *Close Encounters of the Third Kind*.

The skeptics were quick to attack the film. To begin with, they said, the filming was very sloppy for a trained, military cameraman. The two "surgeons" were equally unprofessional – one was even seen to be holding a scalpel incorrectly. Then there was the "alien" itself. Some Hollywood special-effects men insisted that the body was a clever latex model. Others, rather more ghoulishly, suggested it was the dead and disguised body of a human child. In any case, the film irritatingly missed out all the parts of the operation that might have proved instructive to those interested in comparative human/alien anatomy.

Mr Santilli has never claimed that the film is definitely authentic. His reply to the critics was that he bought the film in good faith and that his own researches have shown the filmstock is genuine 1947 Kodak. As of this writing (spring 1997), the debate remains undecided.

In earlier chapters, we have considered the possibility that creatures like fairies and Bigfoot could be explained in terms of hallucination or imagination; but the same explanation cannot be applied to thousands of Goatsucker and cattle mutilation incidents. As with the crop circle enigma, attempts by skeptics to explain them away sound increasingly lame. Oddly enough, John Keel does not believe that the events around Point Pleasant were the work of extraterrestrials, or even the US Government. In his opinion they represent a sort of haunting. He stresses the physical impossibility of many of these happenings – such as a seven-foot, headless humanoid who can fly without moving its wings – and reaches the logical conclusion that they cannot be explained in naturalistic terms. Such a conclusion sounds like an abandonment of our power of reason. Yet the facts speak for themselves. Keel quotes a farmer who claims to have seen men in white overalls attacking her livestock, and when she went after them with a shotgun, they escaped by making an impossible leap over a high fence from a standing start. A similar story is told by Jerome Clark and D. Scott Rogo in *Earth's Secret Inhabitants*. On August 5, 1976, two residents of Atwood,

Colorado watched as two "strange men" started to mutilate a cow. They gave chase, but when the pair seemed to be trapped by a barbed wire fence, they simply vanished into thin air, leaving no footprints or any other physical evidence.

Keel's conclusion, after years of research, is that anomalous events such as the Mothman "haunting", cattle mutilations and UFO sightings represent intrusions into our world by creatures, like "Apol", who naturally exist outside our space-time limitations, but are capable of bridging the barrier into our world. (As we saw in chapter 3, the British investigator F. W. Holiday also came to this conclusion after extensive studies around Loch Ness.) But perhaps we should not regard these incursions as attacks, but simply as explorations of another realm, like man's study of the ocean's depths. Keel points out that "when you review the ancient references you are obliged to conclude that the presence of these [ultraterrestrial] objects and beings is *a normal condition for the planet.*" (his italics).

Even for those willing to believe in alien life, the bizarre events described in this chapter offer no clue to its form or purpose. Dead cattle and goats drained of blood are simply raw data, and that data is meaningless since it has no apparent structure. In *The Mothman Prophecies*, Keel quotes Isaac Asimov: "I am told, though, that so many people have seen objects that looked like spaceships that 'there must be something in it' . . . . Maybe there is, but think of all the people in the history of the world who have seen ghosts and spirits and angels. It's not what you see that is suspect, but how you interpret what you see." Unfortunately, at present, we lack the paradigm that could offer us a clue to the meaning of what we see.

6

Alien Abduction

In 1977, Steven Spielberg's Close Encounters of the Third Kind, *popularised the idea of human-alien contact as only a blockbuster movie can. The special effects, and especially the gray-skinned, almond-eyed aliens, were carefully based on the descriptions of those who claim to be "contactees", yet one aspect of the film – the aliens' benevolent, if enigmatic, demeanor – struck many of these witnesses as false. It was their impression that the creatures from UFOs were cold, unsympathetic or even downright malignant.*

As we saw in the last chapter, some ufologists believe that aliens are behind the hideous mutilation of cattle that has taken place across the globe over at least three decades. In this chapter we look at extraterrestrial dealings with humans and wonder if we should "watch the skies" in hope or fear.

One of the most famous of all cases of UFO "contacts" is the story of Barney and Betty Hill. On September 19, 1961, the couple began their drive from the Canadian border down through New Hampshire, returning from a holiday. Theirs was a mixed marriage, Barney being black and Betty white; they had both been Civil Rights workers.

As they drove along, Betty noticed that a bright object near the moon, which she had assumed to be a star or planet, was getting bigger. When she pointed it out to Barney, he commented that it was probably an artificial satellite. Now, as they drove south through deserted country, the object appeared to be keeping up with them, travelling to the right of their car. It was blinking with multicolored lights. Finally, it was so close that it seemed to be huge, and the blinking lights had changed to a white glow. Finally, Barney stopped the car, and gazed at it through the binoculars. The object was now enormous, and they could see that it had a double row of windows. Barney stopped the car in the middle of the road and got out. Standing at the side of the road, he could see through the windows of the craft, and observed at least half a dozen people who appeared to be staring down at him. Then all but one of them left the windows. Suddenly Barney had a conviction that he was about to be captured, and turned and ran for the car. As they accelerated away down the road, they could see no sign of the UFO. Barney suspected this was because the craft was directly overhead.

At this point they began to hear an electronic beeping noise which made the car vibrate. Suddenly both began to feel a curious sense of drowsiness, followed by a kind of dull haze. When they recovered from this drowsiness, they saw a signpost pointing to Concord, which was seventeen miles away. Neither of them registered the fact that Concord was thirty-five miles away from Indian Head, where they had seen the UFO.

When they arrived home in Portsmouth, the dawn was rising, and their watches had both stopped. But their kitchen clock showed that it was five o'clock. They ate a light breakfast and went straight to bed. The next day, Barney was inclined to dismiss the whole thing, and became annoyed when Betty insisted on talking about it.

To check whether the car had picked up any kind of radiation, Betty approached it with a compass, and was surprised to find on the lid of the boot a dozen or more shiny circles. When the compass was brought close to them, its needle showed a strong reaction. In spite of Barney's protests, she rang a local Air Force base, and told her story – Barney was reluctantly brought to the phone to tell his own version. The officer to whom they spoke was able to tell them that they had received a number of other reports of unidentified flying objects in the area.

Betty went to the local library and borrowed a book called *The Flying Saucer Conspiracy* by Major Donald Keyhoe, which argued that the Air Force was actively trying to discredit all UFO sightings. Keyhoe had organised the National Investigations Committee on Aerial Phenomena in Washington, to correlate and analyse every available UFO sighting. Betty wrote Major Keyhoe a letter, describing their experience – and describing the craft they had seen: "It appeared to be pancake in shape, ringed with windows in the front through which we could see bright blue-white lights. Suddenly, two red lights appeared on each side. By this time my husband was standing in the road, watching closely. He saw wings protrude on either side and the red lights were on the wings' tips."

As a consequence of her letter, the Hills were visited by Walter Webb, a lecturer on the staff of the Hayden Planetarium in Boston. Webb was thoroughly sceptical when he set out on the drive, but after interviewing the Hills for several hours, he was totally convinced that they were telling the truth. Webb subsequently reported to the National Investigations Committee (NICAP) that he was totally convinced that their experience was genuine.

It was when they were repeating their story to a team of three men from NICAP that Barney and Betty Hill became clearly aware that a large section of time seemed to be missing from their drive that night. It was the time between the first occasion when they heard the beeping noise (which induced sleepiness) to the time they again heard the same beeping noise, and noticed the signpost pointing to Concord. The NICAP investigators suggested that it might be worthwhile placing the Hills under hypnosis to see whether they could somehow remember this lost period of time.

During the next year, the Hills returned several times to Indian Head in an attempt to remember precisely what had happened. Always, they ran up against the same amnesia after hearing the first series of beeps. Betty began to suffer from appalling nightmares, while Barney began to show signs of increasing nervous strain. It was after relating their story to a church discussion group in September 1963 that the Hills finally decided to consult a well known Boston psychiatrist, Doctor Benjamin Simon.

On January 4, 1964, Barney Hill was placed under hypnosis by Doctor Simon and taped. Now he was able to remember what had happened after the first series of beeps. Their car had been blocked by a group of humanoids with large eyes, no nose, and slitty lipless mouths. Barney said they reminded him of red-haired, round-faced Irishmen. They were both taken on board the spacecraft – apparently in a kind of trance – and made to lie down on operating tables. Betty had to remove her dress, and a large needle was inserted into her navel –

one of the humanoids, speaking English, told her that he was testing her for pregnancy.

The humanoids seemed very curious about human beings – they wanted to know precisely what they ate and drank, and were intrigued by the fact that Barney's teeth came out whereas hers did not. Finally, they were taken back to their car, and the spacecraft took off. It glowed with an orange color, then rolled "like a ball" and vanished into the dark sky.

On the tape, the Hills are at first able to remember exactly what has happened, and Betty asks her husband "well, now try to tell me you don't believe in flying saucers." But north of Concord, their memory blurs and then vanishes. Oddly enough, although the accounts by Barney and Betty Hill were basically identical, Doctor Simon concluded that their description of going on board the spacecraft was purely imaginary, induced by their alarm at seeing a UFO. (Pease Air Force Base reported that radar had shown a UFO in the air at about the time that the Hills had their encounter.)

Barney Hill died of a cerebral haemorrhage in 1969. Betty Hill continued to reject the notion that what had happened on board the spacecraft was pure imagination.

In the late 1970s, New York painter and sculptor Budd Hopkins became increasingly interested in the phenomenon of "Missing Time" – the gap in people's memories often following a UFO sighting. To begin with, Hopkins was among those who felt that Betty and Barney Hill were unconscious self deceivers. Although he had himself had a daylight UFO sighting in 1964, he simply found himself unable to accept the idea of alien abduction. "Using Justice Frankfurter's distinction, it was not that I thought the Hills were lying, it was just that I could not believe them." Many psychiatrists believe that the Hills had somehow created the fantasy of being abducted while they were under hypnosis, and then come to accept it as real.

Those who claim to be victims of alien abduction often insist that the experience has shattered their lives. They say that they suffer nightmares, anxiety attacks and bizarre health problems – but at least the aliens brought them back. Others have not been so lucky.

On November 23, 1953, Lieutenant Felix Moncla was flying an F-89 interceptor over Lake Superior, when he spotted a UFO and gave chase. As radar operators later asserted, the two blips converged on their screens, merged for a second, then both vanished. Searchers failed to find any trace of either Moncla or his jet.

Strangely enough, the usually thorough Air Force investigation team's report on the incident was only two pages long, and one of those was simply a section copied from a book debunking UFO sightings.

Yet, little by little, his investigation of UFO sightings led him to accept the possibility of alien abduction. In 1981, together with UFO researcher Ted Bloecher and psychologist Doctor Aphrodite Clamar, he wrote the book *Missing Time*, in which he speculated that many people – perhaps thousands – may have had UFO abduction experiences and yet consciously remembered nothing about them. "The pattern of evidence we had uncovered suggests that a kind of 'enforced' amnesia can efficiently erase from conscious memory all but the very slightest recollection of such experiences.

"In one of the seven similar cases we investigated, 'Steven Kilburn' described nothing more than a deep-seated fear of a certain stretch of highway and his 'feeling' that something had happened to him there that possibly involved a UFO. Unlike Betty and Barney Hill he did not recall sighting a UFO, he was not aware of any missing time, or even of seeing anything unusual. But after investigating his case with the help of Ted Bloecher, two psychologists and a polygraph operator, I came to the conclusion that his sketchy, though emotion-loaded, initial recollections did in fact conceal a full-blown UFO abduction experience. Under hypnosis Steve relived a traumatic encounter very similar in its details to the Hill case."

Budd Hopkins reached a startling conclusion. "It appears that most UFO abductees have had more than one such experience, their first abduction generally occurring in childhood around the age of six or seven. Often they are picked up and examined several times after that, though these later encounters are rarely reported past the age of forty or so. An analogy which immediately springs to mind is the human study of endangered animals, in which zoologists tranquilise and tag or implant transmitters in sample animals to trace their subsequent wanderings. I presented evidence in my book indicating a similar interest by UFO 'occupants' in certain human beings who are apparently treated like experimental subjects requiring reexamination at intervals across the years. And as we shall see, there is evidence that these human subjects have also been somehow tagged.

"A third point dealt with the issue of the still-visible

Drawing of the flying saucer sighted by 13-year-old
Stephen Darbishire

scars which apparently resulted from the UFO occupants systematic, quasi-medical examinations of three people when they were first abducted as children. In the illustration section I reproduced three photographs of these small, straight scars as they currently appeared, respectively, on the back of the calf, above the knee, and on the hip of the three different abductees. (By profession they are a corporation lawyer, a microbiologist and a news media employee.) As in the Hill case, hypnosis was used to break the memory blocks and to elicit descriptions of the "surgical" procedures which caused the cuts, as well as detailed recollections of the occupants' physical appearance and of the interiors of the UFOs themselves. Though we do not have any indication of the purpose of these incisions, their physical character suggests a cell-sampling operation of some kind. Over the past five years I have encountered twenty-seven more abductees who bear similarly acquired scars, although a number of these marks are of a different type. Instead of a short, straight cut, seven are circular, shallow depressions – scoop marks, one might say – about a quarter to one half inch in diameter."

As a result of reading *Missing Time*, a woman that Hopkins calls Kathie Davis wrote to him via his publisher. When Hopkins opened her letter, he found fifteen or so color photographs. "I recognised immediately a familiar image from UFO 'landing trace' investigations – a circular area of ground in which all the grass appears to be dead, as if it has been subject to heat or some other form of radiation."

The experience of Kathie Davis was like that of many other people who have encountered UFOs. She described how, in July 1983, she was about to go out one evening to a neighbor's house when she noticed that the pool house door was open and a light was on. As she had closed it earlier, she mentioned this to her mother before she left. Neither of them was unduly alarmed. Checking again just before she went out, she discovered that the light was now off, the pool house door closed, but the garage door was open – it was always kept shut.

From the neighbor's house, she called her mother and discovered that her mother had seen a "big light" by the pool house, and that it had moved to a bird feeder on the lawn and grown to about two feet in diameter. She described it as being like a spotlight trained on the bird feeder. Kathie Davis went home, and searched the property. All she found was her dog hiding under a car. The neighbor and her daughter later came back with her and they went swimming. "Right after that night our yard was burned, by what we don't know. Nothing will grow there now, no matter how much water we give it, and wild animals won't go on it . . . . birds will no longer go near the bird feeder either, and we have always had tons of birds every day, especially rare birds."

The first thing that struck Hopkins was that the "burning" of the grass indicated that some kind of landing had taken place, even though neither Kathie nor her mother could remember anything about it.

The photographs showed a large circle, about eight feet in diameter, on the lawn in which all the grass had turned brown. Extending from this circle was a forty-nine-foot path which ran nearly perfectly straight and was about three feet in width. The grass on this path was also dead.

Kathie Davis went on to tell him about her sister Laura,

a "realist, very level-headed and not much imagination", who was passing a church when she felt compelled to pull into the parking lot at the back. There she looked up, and saw something silver hovering over the lot, at about the height of a telephone pole, with red, green and white lights flickering on and off. "All she remembers now is she reached over to turn down her radio to see if it made noise, and then the next thing she remembers is its dark out and she looks up and this thing is gone and she's driving down the street."

Kathie Davis described another of her sister's curious experiences. Ten years after the car park experience, she went to a hypnotist to try to lose weight, but it seemed to have the opposite effect on her. In the night after the hypnosis, she woke up and found that she was deaf and dumb. Her husband had to take her to hospital, where she was given tranquilisers. It took some time to improve. Moreover, far from wanting to eat less, she found that eating made her feel much better. When she called the hypnotist to ask him why this should be so, the sound of his voice caused her to feel so violent that she wanted to kill him. Laura was left, with one strong thought: "that by the year 2000 the world would be totally different than we know it, but it would be only for the young and strong."

Kathie ended her letter by commenting that both she and her mother had similar scars on their right legs. "I don't remember when I got mine, but it seems like I had it all my life . . . . At first I only had one scar but now I have two, on the same leg."

Budd Hopkins was naturally intrigued. Laura's experience with a hypnotist suggested that the hypnosis had somehow reawakened the abduction experience that

(Hopkins guessed) had taken place in the church car-park.

In a telephone conversation, Kathie told Hopkins of a disturbing dream she had had shortly after her marriage at the age of nineteen. She was facing two strange, gray-faced creatures who stood by her bed. One of them was holding a small black box with a gleaming red light on it. The two moved forward in total unison, and one of them handed her the box. The creatures, she said, had large heads and almost gray skin, and their eyes were "pitch black in color, liquid-like, shimmering in the dim light."

The "creature" then told her that at some time in the future, she would see the box again, and then remember it and "you'll know how to use it." The dream, she said, seemed "utterly real."

Hopkins asked her if she had ever actually *seen* a UFO, and she then described how, as a teenager, she had been driving with two girlfriends in a car when they saw a flashing light in the sky. Somebody said "It's a UFO", and then, as it came closer, "we all got a creepy feeling." They stopped the car to look at it. Kathie could not remember what happened then, so Hopkins asked her if she would call on her friend, Dorothy, and ask her what *she* remembered of the experience. Kathie was surprised when Dorothy remembers even more than she did. Dorothy recalled stopping the car and getting out to look at a light on the ground. Kathie had no memory of getting out of the car. But when she woke up the next morning, she realised that she had arrived home around dawn, and that several hours of the night seemed to be missing.

When he asked Kathie to look more closely at the circular mark on her lawn, Kathie discovered, about two feet beyond the edge of the circle, four small holes, about three inches deep, which could have been made by some sort of landing gear.

Later, Hopkins was to travel to Kathie's home at Copley Woods, near Indianapolis, and interview not only Kathie's mother, but the friend with whom she had spent the evening sewing, Dee Anne, and her eleven-year-old daughter Tammy. Both Dee Anne and Tammy seem to have shared some strange experience that night. Tammy describes feeling nauseated when she went into the pump-house to change into her costume. Dee Anne said that from the moment she arrived in Kathie's back yard she felt uneasy, "like somebody's watching us." Kathie then described how, as they were swimming in the pool, all three of them suddenly felt freezing cold, although the temperature of the air around them was about 80 degrees. Kathie's eyes began to hurt, and things began to look oddly hazy. Also, all began to feel sick at the same time. For some reason, they decided that they ought to eat, and drove to a nearby fast food restaurant, but when they arrived felt so sick that they decided to go straight home.

Neighbors of Kathie Davis – whom Hopkins calls Joyce and Bernie Lloyd – also realised that something odd was going on. Joyce had seen a sudden flash from the direction of Kathie's back yard, followed by a low vibrating sound which caused the house to shake and the chandelier to swing. As the noise increased, the television picture turned red and the lights in the house dimmed and flickered. The sound stopped, and Joyce found herself wondering if she'd been through an earthquake. Bernie Lloyd described how he came home shortly after all this, and found his wife deeply upset.

Later, Hopkins was to interview Joyce Lloyd, and to discover that she was apparently another abductee. Like so many of them, she had a scar on her leg similar to those on the legs of Kathie and her mother. She could only tell Hopkins that it dated from her childhood, but that its origin was unknown. Then she told him of how, when she was driving home in 1981 from a visit to her mother's, she suddenly found herself becoming confused and disoriented. She pulled off the road, and then was unable to remember anything more until she arrived home to find her phone ringing. It was her mother, who always rang her home after she had been there visiting, just to check that she had arrived home safely. On this evening, she was an hour late, but had no idea why.

She had also had a strange experience in the summer of 1984. She had awakened in the middle of the night to find herself upside down in bed, with her feet – which were wet – on her pillow. She was wearing shorts and a t-shirt, which were also damp. She had no recollection of going to bed. But she could remember a dream just before she woke up, in which she had been lying in a field, and had seen a light rising into the sky from the edge of the field. She thought she had seen some kind of "car" in the field, but later said that it was much bigger than a car.

Kathie herself was understandably nervous about these experiences, and wondered what would happen next. Hopkins soothingly reassured her – telling her that UFO experiences generally stopped when investigators like himself began to look into them. Unfortunately, he proved to be wrong. Kathie was due to travel to New York to see him on October 13, 1983, but ten days before this, she had been lying in bed when she heard her name called quite clearly. She felt it was inside her head rather than outside. She immediately rushed to the phone – in the early hours of the morning – and rang a friend of Budd Hopkins called Sue, who had agreed to be "on call" in case anything happened. After this, she awoke her mother, who advised her to take some aspirin and try to get to sleep. Kathie picked up her three-year-old son Tommy, and carried him into her bedroom. As she sat watching the television, she found herself becoming increasingly drowsy, and fell asleep.

Some time later, she was awakened by her mother, who thought that she had heard someone call her name. Kathie said she had been asleep. At that moment, they heard a humming noise from outside the house, rather like a truck with its engine running. Her mother could see nothing out of the window, and finally, they all went back to sleep. But in the morning, Kathie felt completely exhausted, and had a curious stiffness in her arms, shoulders and neck, "as if she'd spent the night lifting weights." Her mother had the same symptoms. When Kathie looked at the bedclothes, she found there were tiny bloodstains on the sheet close to the place where her neck would have rested. There were also stains where her lower back would have rested.

The New York trip went ahead as planned, with Kathie sleeping on a spare bed in Hopkins's studio. She told him that she had suffered various health problems ever since she was very young. She had begun to menstruate at the age of seven, and by the age of ten had high blood pressure. At fourteen, her gall bladder was removed. She suffered from hepatitis and almost died of pneumonia. She had her appendix removed, and once spent two weeks in traction because two vertebrae in her back had somehow fused. The odd thing was that these were extra vertebrae which normal people do not have. In 1983 she had an asthmatic attack. Not long before the experience that led her to write to Hopkins, her heartbeat became so irregular that she needed medical attention. Hopkins suspected that this long list of illnesses might be connected with some psychological tension due to an abduction experience when she was very young.

When Kathie was fourteen, a small bump appeared on the front of her shin, and she found that she could move it around with her fingers. When she went into hospital for the gall bladder operation, the doctor said he would remove it while she was under the anaesthetic. When she woke up, he showed her a small, bone-like object, and told how, when he sliced into her skin with his scalpel, this had shot straight up several feet into the air, hitting the metal reflector of the surgical lamp with a ping. Unfortunately, Kathie had not kept this cyst.

But Kathie had had an even stranger and more ominous experience. As a teenager, she had been sexually experimental. In 1977, when she was eighteen, she met the man who was to become her husband. Early the following year, she realised that she was pregnant. Medical tests confirmed the pregnancy. They decided to move the wedding forward a few months. Then, one morning in March, she woke up finding herself menstruating normally. A visit to the doctor confirmed the fact that she was no longer pregnant. Yet there had been no obvious miscarriage or traces of a natural abortion. She had simply ceased to be pregnant. Kathie was placed under hypnosis by Hopkins's associate Doctor Clamar. During the first session, she recounted how she had wakened in the middle of the night in 1978, and seen two small, gray-faced figures standing by her bed.

At the next session, she went on to describe further how she awoke in bed with her husband, gone to the kitchen, then stood by the sink as if waiting for something. After that, she felt herself floating, with her eyes closed, through the air. Next, she found herself lying down, and seemed to be in the process of being physically examined. She felt two thin probes pressing up her nose, and they seemed to break through the skin in the region of her sinuses. She felt the taste of something like blood. After this, she felt pressure on her abdomen, then on her neck. When she opened her eyes, she saw a small, gray-faced man standing next to the table on which she lay. There was a moment of panic, as the man's "huge black eyes" looked down at her, then she felt suddenly reassured. After this, she seemed to awaken in bed with the two gray figures standing beside them, holding a kind of shimmering box. One of them handed her the box – as in her previous dream – and told her that when she saw it again, she would understand its purpose. After this, she fell asleep.

At this point, Hopkins breaks off his narrative to describe parallel cases. A girl from Kentucky had described to him how, as a five-year-old child, she had been taken by "little men" into some kind of cold, brightly lit craft, and placed on a table. She was unable to move, and after this, something was inserted up her nose. In another case, a woman from Texas who had been involved in an abduction incident described how some probe had been inserted up her nose with a tiny ball on the end. Hopkins suspected that the ball was somehow left behind after the operation – in other words, that it was some kind of "implant". Hopkins was also intrigued by the fact that the two gray figures appeared to move in absolute unison, and recalled how another abductee who had encountered five tall figures on a lonely road noticed that they all seemed to move simultaneously as they walked towards him. Hopkins comments: "I not know what this clonelike appearance and behavior means, but it is not a constant in abduction reports."

Further investigation of the incident on October 3, when Kathie woke up believing that she heard someone call her name, proved that there had been earlier "incidents". Before she had gone to bed, she drove to a nearby all-night food store to get something to drink. When she returned, she realised that she had still not bought anything to drink. She turned and drove back – and at this point, saw a large, brightly-lit object in the sky that she assumed was some kind of advertising balloon. It was rolling in a hypnotic manner. After this, she thought she went into the store, but the man she saw there was not like the clerk who usually served her. In fact, she now recognized that the store was not a store, but some kind of spacecraft. And so, apparently, Kathie had had another "abduction experience" ten days before she came to New York – and was only able to recollect it under hypnosis. Moreover, she remembered how, after she had fallen asleep in bed, her whole body began to tingle, and she felt herself being examined again.

Back in Copley Woods, she was awakened one night by an awful scream coming from the children's room. Her son Robbie was lying awake, looking shocked. When Kathie told him he must have had a bad dream, he replied "Mommy, this ain't no dream." He told her that a man with a big head had come in through the wall and went into her closet, "and he wouldn't let me move." The man told him that he wanted his brother Tommy. She went back to the children's bedroom to look at Tommy, and thought that she saw a flash of light coming from the closet. When she looked, there was nothing there.

A week later, she went into the children's bedroom in the morning, and found Tommy covered with blood. In the hospital, the doctors told her that Tommy had apparently suffered a massive nose bleed in the night – without waking up. An examination of the child's nostrils revealed a small hole high up in his sinus. The doctor thought that Tommy must have pushed a pencil – or some similar object – up his nose.

When Kathie phoned him to tell him about this, Hopkins immediately found himself thinking about the other abductees who had had things inserted up their noses, and suspected that, on the first night when Robbie had seen the man with the big head – the man who said he had "come for Tommy" – Tommy had been "anaesthetised" and some kind of implant placed in his nose. Hopkins suspected that this implant had come out a week later, causing the bad nose bleed.

Hopkins also recalled another of his abductee subjects who, at the age of five, was awakened when she heard her name called. She was told to go to the kitchen, where she saw three men in uniforms standing outside the back door. The door opened without anyone touching it, and the men – who had "bad eyes and no mouth" – picked her up and carried her out. She was taken into a large, metallic object, subjected to some kind of physical examination, and then taken back to her bed. When

115

she woke the next morning, her pyjamas were covered with dried blood – she had had a violent nose bleed in her sleep, so violent that it had clotted the braids of her hair and pooled in her ears.

In 1986, more than two years after Tommy's violent nose bleed, Robbie came into his mother's bedroom and told her there was" a red tarantula" on the wall of his room. Assuming he had been dreaming, Kathie pulled the bedclothes over him and he went to sleep. But as she lay there in bed watching television, she saw a small, grayskinned figure walk straight past the open door. He appeared to be coming from the children's room.

Another strange event had occurred soon after Tommy's nose bleed. She dreamed that she was lying on a table with her nightgown pulled up under her breasts while the little man with big eyes examined her. He asked her – telepathically – how she was feeling, and when she said she felt tired and "kind of crampy" he patted her gently on the stomach and said: "That's good." After this, she went back to sleep. But the next morning, she was baffled to find that her panties were lying on top of the bedcovers. She had gone to bed wearing them underneath her nightgown, and certainly had no memory of removing them during the night. That day, she felt pain in her lower abdomen, in the region of her left ovary. It proved to be the day that she was expecting to menstruate. Hopkins suspected that the ovum had been taken from her the previous night.

Now, little by little, these strange events were beginning to come together into a pattern, and Hopkins was disturbed by what he suspected. He happened to know something about the famous abduction experience of Betty and Barney Hill. Although it had not been published

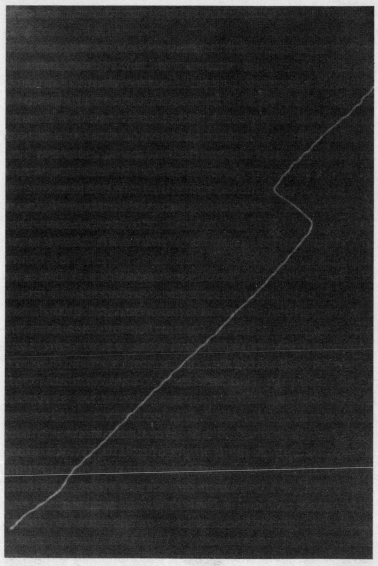

Trail made by a UFO sighted in Austin, Texas, October 1974

in John Fuller's book *The Interrupted Journey*, Barney Hill had described how, during the abduction, a sperm sample was taken from him. And Betty, of course, had described having a long needle inserted into her navel. At that time, no such "needle" was in use in hospitals. But ten years or so later, there was now a device called a lamaroscope – a long, flexible tube containing fibre optics – that could be inserted into the patient's navel for looking inside her, and also for removing ova for fertilisation as so called "test tube babies".

Hopkins was also reminded of the curious experience of Antonio Villas-Boas, the young Brazilian farmer who claimed to have been taken on board a UFO, and being virtually raped by some kind of female alien. "As the cases have slowly accumulated, the patterns have become clearer. Over the past six years I have worked with four male abductees who have described encounters very similar to Villas-Boas's abduction, and three others whose incomplete account strongly suggests such an event. The female side of this equation, which we will examine later on, is more complex. It should be pointed out, however, that I know of *no* case in which a female abductee has ever reported an act of intercourse. Above all, in none of these cases involving either men or women do we have what can be called a basically *erotic* experience. The descriptions are invariably of a detached, clinical procedure instead, even if some of them result in more or less involuntary ejaculation.

"Now all of this leads to the unwelcome speculative inference that somewhere, somehow, human beings – or possibly hybrids of some sort – are being produced by a technology obviously – yet not inconceivably – superior to ours. And if that possibility is not enough to induce paranoia in the heartiest, consider this: With our own current technology of genetic engineering expanding day by day, is it not conceivable that an advanced alien technology may already have the ability to remove ovum and sperm from human beings, experimentally alter their genetic structure, and then *replant* altered and fertilised ova back into unknowing host females to be carried to term? Ova that can be removed can also be replaced, even by our own present-day medical technology."

In short, Hopkins suspects that what is happening is that female abductees are being artificially inseminated, possibly by male sperm taken from other abductees, allowed to carry the foetus for some time, and then subjected to another operation which removes the foetus.

When Hopkins visited Kathie in Copley Woods, she said something that confirmed this suspicion. When he remarked how lucky she was to have two boys like Tommy and Robbie, she stopped the car and said: "Budd, you know I have a daughter too." She went on, "I know I have a daughter. I think I've even seen her. I know what she looks like."

It was when Kathie visited New York for a second time that Hopkins realised that one of the earlier incidents she had described was more significant than it seemed. Kathie had earlier described how, as a teenager, she was driving around late at night with two girlfriends when they saw a UFO. At this point, Kathie's memory seemed to blur, and all she could remember was feeling "frozen" in the car, unable to move. Her friend Dorothy seemed to have a memory of getting out of the car, and then could both remember their friend Roberta crouching in the back seat and refusing to look. After this, Kathie had arrived home far later than she expected. Under hypnosis, Kathie remembered this event in more detail. It was at the time that she had just met her future husband. Now, under hypnosis, Kathie was able to remember how they sat looking up at the light in the sky, until it seemed to be right over them, looking like "an airplane with the strobe things on it." After this there was a flash in the car, and Kathie describes how she suddenly became very cold. Everything became black, and she wanted to get out of the car, but was unable to move. She explained that her back felt stiff and that her arms and legs felt cold and heavy. She seemed to be held down by an invisible force. Finally, she recollects getting out of the car, and standing beside Dorothy, watching something float off into the sky.

At this point in the hypnosis, Hopkins took her back to the flash in the car. He suspected that Kathie had been abducted first, and then returned to the car, after which her friend Dorothy was abducted. In fact, Kathie now began to remember some kind of pain that "makes my stomach hurt. It feels like my legs are being pulled off my body from the waist down." As Kathie moans in pain, Hopkins asks her where the pain is situated. "Where my uterus is, down low, like I'm going to have my period. It's hard, it hurts. It's like a toothache . . . . Oh it feels like someone's pushing on me *real hard* . . . . Wiggling and pushing right in there." She explains that it feels like "a finger" right above her bladder.

This, Hopkins came to believe, was the point at which she was artificially impregnated. And the baby was taken away in the following March, when she woke up and found herself menstruating. Later, still under hypnosis, Kathie described how she was again lying on a couch, apparently undergoing some kind of pelvic examination. Suddenly, she told Hopkins, "I just want to scream." When he asks if she means scream from the pain, she suddenly says in a high wailing voice, "No! It's not right, it's not fair! IT'S NOT FAIR! IT'S MINE! IT'S MINE! I HATE YOU. I HATE YOU! . . . . IT'S NOT FAIR!" This, Hopkins realised, was the moment when her baby was taken away.

Later still, Kathie explained what she meant when she had said that she had a daughter and that she had seen her. She had awakened in a place that was "all white", and that there were several of these "little gray guys" around her. She was standing up, and one of them had his arm around her waist, as if to comfort her. At this point, a little girl came into the room, escorted by two of the gray men. "She looked to be about four. She looked about Tommy's size . . . . She was real pretty. She looked like an elf, or an . . . . angel. She had really big blue eyes and a little teeny-weeny nose, just so perfect. And her mouth was just so perfect and tiny, and she was pale, except her lips were pink and her eyes were blue. And her hair was white and wispy and thin . . . . fine . . . . real thin and fine. Her head was a little larger than normal, 'specially not in the forehead and back here . . . . The forehead was a little bit bigger . . . . but she was just a doll. And they brought her to me. And they stood there, and they looked at me. Everyone was looking at me. And I looked at her, and I wanted to hold her. She was just so pretty, and I felt like I just wanted to hold her. And I started crying . . . ." Before the grey men took the child away, they told Kathie that she would see her again.

Under hypnosis, she was able to recollect how the little gray man whom she thought of as the child's "father" held her hand, "and I feel all kinds of things

. . . . sad, and warm, and care, and distance . . . . and goodbye . . . . and lonely . . . . I feel lonely too."

When she was awake, she expanded on this final experience. "You know, when he looked at me and held my hand I got this rush of emotion that I didn't know where it came from. It was lonely and sad and sorry, but love and caring and happiness and satisfaction – and guilt – all at once. I didn't think it was coming from me. Why would I feel guilt?" Hopkins said that perhaps it was his guilt she was aware of. "Yes, it wasn't my guilt. He felt sad and lonely, but he felt satisfied and happy, and he cared, about me, as a living thing. He was going to miss me as much as I was going to miss her." She adds, "he wanted me to be happy at the success like he was, and he felt guilty that I felt that way . . . ."

This, then, is Hopkins thesis. The "aliens" – little gray men with large heads and big black eyes – are somehow using human beings to create hybrids. In a chapter called "Other Women, Other Men", he goes on to describe a number of other cases that seem to echo the one he has already described. A subject called Andrea had told him how she was "floated out of her bed" into a UFO. There, as she sat paralysed on the table, a long needle was pressed up her nose, causing her pain as it broke through the top of her nasal cavity. When she woke up in the morning, there was blood on her nightgown and the bedclothes from a bad nose bleed. Andrea accounted for a scar on her chest by explaining that when she was about six-years-old, she could recall lying on a table in a small, round room lit by pink light, and a small man doing something to her chest. Hopkins's female assistant Louise later saw a thin red cut three-and-a-half inches long down the centre of Andrea's back.

Were aliens involved in World War II? It may sound bizarre, but there does appear to be some evidence for the proposition, although which side they backed, if any, remains open to question.

In late 1944, Reuters' news agency reported that the Germans had developed aircraft that resembled "the glass balls that adorn Christmas trees. They have been seen hanging in the air over German territory, sometimes singularly, sometimes in clusters. They are colored silver and are apparently transparent."

Allied pilots saw these unidentified flying objects often enough to give them a nickname – Foo Fighters (from the French word *Feu*, meaning fire). They were commonest over Germany, but were also seen over neutral Turkey and as far field as Japan.

The Allied intelligence services made great efforts to find out what the Germans were up to but, despite having by then thoroughly infiltrated the Nazi war machine, they got nowhere. After VE day, the German files were searched and experimental bases ransacked, but no reference to the strange globes could be found.

The US government apparently forgot about the matter very quickly. Two years later, in 1947, people across America were reporting "flying saucers," yet nobody in official circles mentioned the UFO's obvious similarity with the Foo Fighters.

But Andrea had had an even stranger experience. When she was thirteen, and still a virgin, she became pregnant. At this time she did not even have a boyfriend. She dreamed that she was having sex with a man who had no hair on his head and "real funny eyes".

"I just felt something in me, something sharp, and then my vagina felt like it was on fire .... In the morning my underpants were all wet and the bed was wet, and I felt all burning.

"And after a while my stomach started to grow. My mother took me to a gynecologist, and I was pregnant. I couldn't believe it. My father was furious and asked who did it to me, he wanted to get even. I told him it was a weird man in a dream, with funny eyes and a big head. And you know, Budd, the gynecologist said I was still a virgin. I still had my hymen."

The situation was resolved when Andrea had an abortion.

Another one of Hopkins's subjects, a girl called Susan, described a similar experience when she was in Austria as a young woman in 1953. She was sixteen at the time, and had stopped her car to watch a strange, darting light in the sky. She then began to feel some kind of telepathic communication between herself and the UFO. She felt herself rising vertically off the road, floating upwards until she came to rest on her back on a table inside the UFO. She was relaxed and unafraid, although she was naked from the waist down. She felt two small clips being attached to her labia, spreading them apart, and then a thin probe moving up inside her. It seems that the purpose of this operation was not to impregnate her, but to examine her internally.

She told Hopkins that a year after this experience, she told her boyfriend about her experience. At this point, Susan decided to ring the boyfriend to see whether he could remember the conversation. In fact, he could not recall it, but *did* remind her of a UFO sighting they had made together at that time. She had totally forgotten about this sighting. As a result of further questioning, Hopkins came to the conclusion that both Susan and her boyfriend had shared an abduction experience at some point. He suspected that, at the age of sixteen, she was impregnated, and that later, that baby was removed.

Another abductee called Pam described under hypnosis how she and her sister had seen a "low, silver-gray vehicle" pull up beside their car when they had broken down, and that her mind had then become confused. Later, when she was married and living in New Mexico, she had a recurrent nightmare involving a "silver train" which was coming down from the sky to take her away. And although she was practising birth control at this time, she suddenly found herself pregnant. Medical tests confirmed this, and she decided to have an abortion. But when she went to the clinic – apparently two months pregnant – the doctor told her that there was no sign whatever that she had ever been pregnant.

Hopkins goes on to describe some curious experiences of male abductees he has interviewed. A man he calls Ed wrote him a letter telling him that he was a roving mechanic at a mine, and that one night, dozing in his truck, he had suddenly found himself "frozen" and unable to move. When he read Hopkins's *Missing Time*, he began to suspect that he had had some kind of UFO experience during this period of paralysis. Under hypnosis, he was able to remember it. He was just about to go to sleep in the truck when a bright light dazzled him. After this, he felt weightless, and floated up through the air. He was taken into a UFO – let in through the door. Its inhabitants, who had round heads and thin features, made him lie down on a table, naked, and then examined him carefully all over. He noticed that they seemed to have a particular interest in his genital region.

The following day, when his wife was not present, Ed told the rest of the story. A woman was brought into the room, "built more like a human being . . . . she had mammaries, but she didn't have any body hair at all. Her head was larger than a normal woman's would be." Ed explained that he was lying on his back, naked, "and somehow they made me erect and she mounted me . . . . she rode me and she was on top of me until I orgasmed, and then she got off and left the room and the two guys, they took little spoons and scraped the leftover semen off my penis and took it as a sample in a bottle and kept it."

Hopkins wanted to know how they had caused him to have an erection, and Ed replied "God, this is preposterous, but it seems they stuck like a vacuum device on my penis." When he came out of his trance, he noticed that his abductors seemed angry – the reason being that he had had a vasectomy two years before, and therefore was sterile.

As a result of telling Hopkins about this experience, Ed recalled an earlier abduction. He had felt a sudden urge to go into the back yard in the middle of the night, and the small men emerged from the woods, and somehow paralysed him. In the UFO, a suction device was put on his penis, and the result was that he reached ejaculation – apparently without any kind of sexual excitement. This may have been the reason that the abductors returned a few years later and took him off for a second sample – only to find that he was now sterile. After this experience, Ed explained that he was left with a deep, aching sensation in the region of his pubic bone. Ed then recalled two earlier abduction experiences, one when he was a child of five, and one when he was a teenager. This leads Hopkins to comment, "One of the major findings described in my book *Missing Time* was an apparent programme of systematically repeated abductions of the same individuals over many years. The analogy mentioned earlier that comes to mind is our programme of zoological study in which wild animals are captured and tranquilised to allow the permanent attachment of small transmitters or even simple tags before they are released back into their natural environments. The transmitters allow scientists to track their movements and thus to learn the species' migration patterns, grazing habits and other useful information. This analogy is obviously anthropomorphic, but it is nevertheless suggested, especially since there is evidence that tiny implants are put in place in UFO abduction cases, as we have seen."

Hopkins goes on to cite the experience of another abductee, a man he calls Dan, a factory worker from Ohio. Dan wrote to Hopkins in some distress, saying that he had had some kind of disturbing experience. When Hopkins finally went to see him, he discovered that Dan's abduction experiences had dated from early childhood.

He had been with a group of people when several of them were taken into a UFO. He describes lying on a table, with his legs spread wide apart, while his abductors "put something on my genital area. It looks kinda clear, a conical shape, it covers up the whole area. There's a sensation, of vibrating. It didn't hurt. I just feel that vibrating, and it seems like a shock. I don't know. Kind of like a pleasant shock . . . . I could feel it touching the end of my penis, and right around the whole area. It felt kinda cold." As he ejaculated, he experienced an odd electrical sensation in his head. Hopkins suggests that this electrical sensation could be some kind of "artificial neurological trigger for the sexual release." He mentions another abductee who had also had some kind of clear plastic covering placed over his genitals, felt a vibration, then the sudden rush of the orgasm, and the sense that his semen had been taken as a sample.

Hopkins also explores the question of the "paralysis" that the abductors seem to be able to induce at will. Kathie Davis had also experienced something of the sort in her teens. She described to Hopkins how she made a trip to Kentucky when she was sixteen with the family of her girlfriend Nan. They had stayed in a cabin at the side of a lake. Nan's father had a Citizen-Band radio in his car, and the girls somehow got into contact with a group of boys who were also using a CB radio. While Kathie was still sitting in front of the radio, the boys – three of them – suddenly arrived in a car. The odd thing was that, although the track was bumpy and pitted, the car seemed to glide as smoothly as if it was on a tarmac road. Kathie was puzzled about how the boys had succeeded in finding them – they had given them no instructions. When she took the three boys indoors – one of them was blonde, and did most of the talking – they discovered that everybody was still awake, in spite of the lateness of the hour. They seemed to be standing there, as if they were waiting for something. The "boys" sat down and drank beer, and the conversation went on for hours. Kathie apparently found the blonde boy extremely attractive. The next day, Kathie and Nan went to the place where the boys claimed they were camping, but found no camping site in the area.

Hopkins was greatly struck by Kathie's description of taking the boys into the cabin. "I was sure some of them would have been in bed, since it was late, but they were all up, just sitting there or standing, and the TV wasn't even on. But Budd, they were just *still*, you know, not moving, like they were hardly awake, and not saying anything. And my head started to feel funny, between my eyes, and then the blonde guy spoke and everyone kind of came to life, and began to move and talk. It was really weird, like they had been asleep or something."

Hopkins summarises some of his conclusions in the final chapter of the book. "And behind the abduction phenomenon as it has been described by literally hundreds of witnesses there seems to be a very peculiar and very consistant ethical position. In none of the cases I've investigated have I ever encountered even the suggestion of deliberate harm or malevolence. The abductees are apparently kept as calm as possible and seem to suffer only minimal physical pain – a situation not unlike that of a well-run dental office. People are picked up, examined, samples are taken and so on, and then they are returned more or less intact to the place where the abduction began. There seems to be a definite effort by the UFO occupants to make the operations as swift, efficient, and painless as possible. There is reason to believe that the partial amnesia which often accompanies these experiences is intended to help the abductees continue their normal lives as much as it is to conceal UFO activities."

And yet, Hopkins points out, most abductees *do* suffer some kind of harm. One woman who had suffered several abduction experiences as a child attempted to kill herself when she was ten. It was only later that she realised that she was suffering a deep sense of dread because of her abduction experiences – which she had consciously forgotten.

Hopkins seems to feel that the abductors are curiously naive. "In one case I've investigated, a Minnesota man and his wife were abducted together; the husband was forced to watch helplessly while a long needle was run into the navel of his paralysed wife. His abductors were completely surprised by his fury and hatred. 'But we *want* you to see what we're doing,' they explained ingenuously. 'We are not harming your mate. Why are you angry?'" It would seem, Hopkins points out, that the aliens are oddly emotionless beings who cannot comprehend why their scientific experiments should upset their human victims. "Their psychology, if one can use the term, does not make any more sense to us than human psychology apparently makes to them." So, according to Hopkins, the abductors are neither evil aliens, bent on destroying the human race, nor benevolent "visitors from space", whose only purpose is to aid the evolution of the human race. Whatever they're doing seems rather more complicated.

Another disturbing aspect is the sheer *number* of such cases. Hopkins describes how, after he appeared on a TV program with two abductees, the station was suddenly flooded with phone calls and letters from people who all suspected that they had been abductees.

Next to Budd Hopkins, the best known investigator of UFO abductions is probably Doctor David M. Jacobs, who is a historian specialising in twentieth century America. Jacobs became interested in UFOs in the early

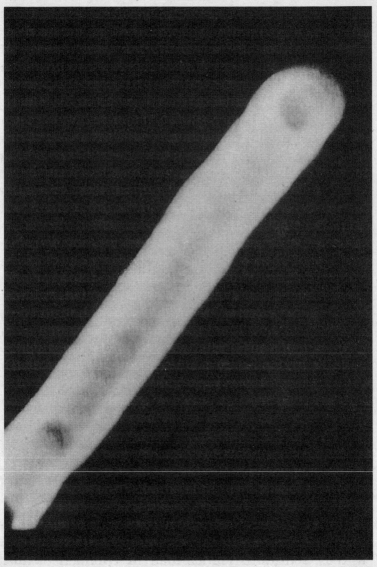

UFO sighted in Palermo, Sicily, 1978

sixties, when he was a student at the University of Wisconsin. When, in 1966, he read John Fuller's *The Interrupted Journey*, about Barney and Betty Hill, he was skeptical – it seemed to him far more likely that the "memories" of abduction had been induced by the hypnosis. As a historian, he was inclined to concentrate on trying to find historical patterns in the phenomena. He at first found the sheer diversity of the reports bewildering – two men who claimed to have been abducted by creatures with skin like elephants and long sharp noses and hands like claws; one who claimed to have been abducted not only by aliens but by a human being as well; a woman who said she had been transported to another planet, and various abductees who reported Benevolent Beings who had come to teach the human race how to live at peace.

The turning point came when he met Budd Hopkins in 1982, and decided that he would have to begin doing hypnotic regression himself. In 1986, he tried his skills on his first abductee – a woman he calls Melissa Bucknell. She had been hypnotised before, so his nervousness was unnecessary – she quickly went into a trance. Then she described how, as a six-year-old child playing in a field near her home, she was transported into a UFO by aliens. Her clothes were removed and a physical examination was performed, including probing her vagina with a needle-like instrument. She felt that something had been implanted near her left ovary.

Soon, Jacobs had a large number of regular "patients", and during the next five years, conducted more than 325 hypnotic sessions. His approach to the question was basically statistical. Rather than describing particular abductions in some detail, like Budd Hopkins, he prefers to list the phenomena under various headings, like "Getting There, Physical Probing, Alien Bonding, and The Breeding Programme." In his book *Secret Life* (1992), published in paperback as *Alien Encounters*, he gives a basic picture of what happens to so many people. "An unsuspecting woman is in her room preparing to go to bed. She gets into bed, reads a while, turns off the light, and drifts into a peaceful night's sleep. In the middle of the night she turns over and lies on her back. She is awakened by a light that seems to be glowing in her room. The light moves towards her bed and takes the shape of a small 'man' with a bald head and huge black eyes. She is terrified. She wants to run but she cannot move. She wants to scream but she cannot speak. The 'man' moves towards her and looks deeply into her eyes. Suddenly she is calmer, and she 'knows' that the 'man' is not going to hurt her." After this, the abductee finds himself or herself floating up through the air, and then into the spacecraft, where he or she is examined on some kind of table, by small creatures with large heads and huge black eyes that slant a little like a cat's. There are also usually some Taller Beings, inches to a foot higher, and who seem to have authority over the smaller beings – like a doctor over nurses; they may intervene if the abductee shows himself to be angry or difficult, or needs to be physically restrained. The room may contain other tables, with other human beings lying on them, usually in a kind of semi-anaesthetised state. One abductee described a hall with about two hundred "beds" in it. A lengthy examination usually follows – not unlike the kind of examination conducted by a doctor for an insurance company – except that it seems to be far more searching.

Jacobs also notes that the aliens seem to indulge in a kind of activity that he calls "Mindscan". This is usually carried out by one of the "Taller Beings". They seem to play a more authoritative role in the process of examination. "Mindscan" involves staring deep into the eye of the abductee, so that the latter feel as if some kind of information has been extracted from their minds. During this process, what Jacobs calls "Bonding" often occurs. This is the feeling that was described by Kathie Davis when she talked to the being she felt to be the "father" of her child – a sense of close kinship. The result is not unlike the "transference" phenomenon in psychotherapy – when the patient falls in love with the doctor and places him on a pedestal. When it happens to small children, they become convinced that the "Taller Being" is a friend who can be totally trusted. One abductee, under hypnosis, described how when she was twelve, she looked into the eyes of one of the "Taller Beings", and experienced a sensation of love in which there was a definite sexual component. "He looked into my eyes, and I really liked him . . . . I just felt happy and I just lay down."

After this, females may experience some kind of implant. One said indignantly, "I feel like a cow. I'm so mad . . . ." When this abductee awoke the next morning in her bed, she found a sticky gelatinous substance between her legs, which she washed off in the shower. Males often experience the kind of "sperm extraction" described by Budd Hopkins. A cup-like machine is placed over the penis, also covering the scrotum. After this, sexual arousal is experienced, while the alien may press or "knead" the right side of the lower abdomen. "That's when I ejaculate . . . . I think while one little guy hooks up the machine the other one pumps my stomach for some reason . . . . when he looks into my eyes, I get this bonding feeling. When the machine's all hooked up and ready, he strokes me or something. It feels pleasurable. And I ejaculate into the machine." Another comments, "There's an erection and there's no sense of release or anything orgasmic; it is just like a literal drawing out." In other words, the sperm-extractor seems to have something in common with a milking machine used on cows.

The aliens also seem to be able to cause imagery to arise in the mind of the abductee, often associated with some powerful emotion – one woman relived the experience of being beside her mother when she was dying of cancer. Another abductee who was subjected to a powerful "envisioning" process said, "They gave me some pretty vivid images . . . . but they didn't do it in that room, they put me in a little room with a chair. Just one chair in the middle . . . . and I sat on the chair and they put this scope on my head. It looked something like what they looked at me in. It's real bright now. It seems like a bright room and they told me terrible things would happen to the Earth and that it would just blow up, and cities would crumble and mountains would fall and the sun would be black. And they said that it's bad because people can't stop being greedy and that they were doing something to help us, and I don't know how . . . . they were horrible images, the images I still see in nightmares. I have recurring nuclear war dreams."

He is asked, "What are they doing while you are receiving these images?" The abductee explains that one of them is holding an instrument like a telescope or kaleidoscope up against his forehead. This, he thought, was to enable the alien to look at images in his mind. And he feels that when the being looks into his eyes, "I think he's looking into my soul." The aliens appear to be able to induce illusions. One female abductee was told to sit down on a couch, in front of a table with a flower-pot on it. A number of human guards were standing around. A male to whom she was very attracted was brought into the room and she was astonished to see him. He came over and leaned forward to kiss her, so that she had the feeling that they were going to make love. But looking around, she suddenly realised that the human guards were actually aliens, and that the male who was about to kiss her was also an alien. The purpose of these "staged" scenes appears to be psychological study of the individual concerned.

Like Kathie Davis, many abductees are brought into contact with alien babies, or foetuses often. The abductee is required to hold a baby and establish some kind of physical contact. One abductee suggested that she thought the purpose of this exercise was to give the alien baby some experience of "touching". Both Hopkins and Jacobs point out that it has been discovered that touching is essential to all babies – animal as well as human. Without touching, normal development can be unsatisfactory and greatly retarded. Jacobs observes the abductee often feels that some of the babies are hers, and that she is a part of some grand scheme, and has reason to feel proud of herself. One male abductee was introduced to a little girl who reminded him of his niece. As she reached up and touched his cheek – "like a little poke" – he experienced a sense of "joining". When the child was taken away, he became deeply upset, although the aliens appeared to find this baffling. Finally, one of the "taller beings" stared at him, and somehow made him calm down.

In one strange procedure, abductees are made to climb into a kind of pool, and they find that they can actually breathe under the liquid, which seems to be more gelatinous than water.

Hopkins's observation that normal sexual activity never seems to occur in abduction situations is contradicted by Jacobs. One young woman described how she was taken to a male abductee, who was lying, apparently unconscious, on the table. The aliens wanted her to get on top of him. In spite of her unwillingness, she was made to climb on to his erection, and move up and down on him until he ejaculated inside her. When she moved off him, he remained erect.

One fifteen-year-old girl had some kind of head gear attached to her, which induced powerful sexual feelings. Since she was inexperienced, she did not understand these. After this, a middle-aged man with a paunch is brought in, his eyes glazed over and unfocussed. One of the "taller beings" makes her body respond sexually after this, "this guy climbs on top of me, and he's moving and it . . . . doesn't make any sense, but it feels like he starts to climax and doesn't finish, or he gets to the point of coming, but what's the point of that? . . . . they just pull him off, and stick something up where he was, a metal thing it feels like." Another thirteen-year-old girl was told that she was now "ripe" and that she should go and breed. After that, they brought in a teenage boy who also seemed to be in a trance, and who climbed on her and ruptured her hymen. This happened to her on two occasions while she was still a teenager.

There are also occasions when the alien has sex with the abductee. In that case, the abductee is somehow made to believe that the person who is making love to her is her husband or someone she loves. The alien's face may change into that of the husband. The insertion of the "penis" is quick, and the penis does not feel normal; it is usually very thin and very short. The normal thrusting movement does not take place, but the woman feels a sudden "pulse". Then it is all over. "We have no clear evidence that the aliens have genitals, but hybrids sometimes do."

In the remainder of his book, Jacobs examines in some detail other aspects of the abduction experience – how the abductee finds himself or herself back home, the appearance and behavior of the aliens, the psychological problems that may result from the abduction, even if the abductee experiences total amnesia about it. Like Hopkins, Jacobs observes how often female abductees experience unplanned pregnancies. The woman is often deeply puzzled and disturbed because she is not engaged in sex, or has taken full birth control precautions. Then, a few months later, the pregnancy suddenly vanishes, with no kind of discharge or miscarriage.

David Jacobs' work is remarkable for its analytical breakdown of the abduction phenomenon, and for the extreme care with which he documents various aspects. Yet at the end of the book, in a kind of question-and-answer session, he answers the question, "Why do aliens repeatedly abduct the same people?" "We do not know the answer to this."

The latest "respectable" addition to the ranks of the UFO researchers is Dr John E. Mack, Professor of Psychiatry at Harvard medical school, and the author of a

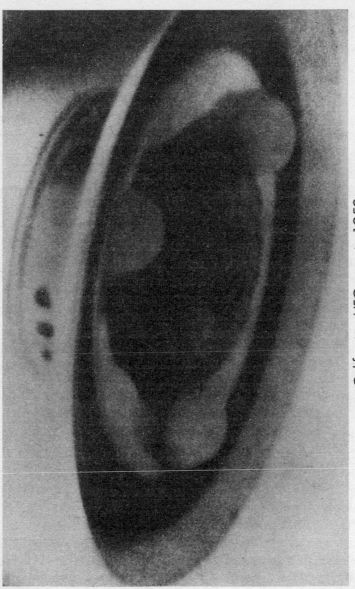

Californian UFO seen in 1952

classic biography of Lawrence of Arabia. At the beginning of his book *Abduction* (1994), he describes how a colleague asked him if he wanted to meet Budd Hopkins, and he replied "Who's he?" When told that Hopkins was a New York artist who interviewed people who claimed to have been abducted by aliens in spaceships, Mack replied that he must be crazy. Finally, in January 1990, he was introduced to Hopkins by his colleague. After Mack had interviewed four abductees, and heard the same stories of their encounters with aliens, he began to conclude that perhaps, after all, they were telling the truth.

After this, Hopkins began to refer him to cases that took place in the Boston area, and during the course of the next three-and-a-half years, he saw over a hundred persons, of whom seventy-six (whose ages ranged from two to fifty-seven) fulfilled his "quite strict criteria for an abduction case: conscious recall or recall with the help of hypnosis, of being taken by alien beings into a strange craft, reported with emotion appropriate to the experience being described and no apparently mental condition that could account for the story." Typical of the cases cited by Mack is that of a twenty-two-year-old music student whom he calls Catherine. In February 1991, she had started to drive home from a nightclub where she worked as receptionist, but experienced an odd desire to go for a drive. When she returned home, she realised that there seemed to be a forty-five minute period for which she could not account. The next day, when she woke up, the television news mentioned that someone had seen a UFO over Boston, and a map of the object's path showed that it seemed to be travelling in the direction in which she had driven. A violent nose bleed – the first of her life – led her to feel that something strange had happened.

Under hypnosis, Catherine recalled that her first abduction experience had happened when she was three-years-old. She was awakened in the middle of the night and saw some "being" at her bedroom window with a blue light streaming in behind it. It had "huge black eyes, a pointed chin – his entire head is like a teardrop inverted. He's got a line for a mouth, nose I can't see . . . . It's just a bump. He doesn't seem to be wearing any clothes." The being came into the room, and Catherine was "floated" through the window and taken to a disc-shaped ship outside. In a large room, with several older children, she was asked by a woman who reminded her of a nursery school teacher whether she wanted to play. The teacher then produced a kind of metallic ball which floated around the room and handed her a metallic rod with a short antenna coming out of the top. This rod was apparently able to control the metal ball, to make it stop or move around or hover, but this also required considerable concentration. Catherine did so well at it that she sensed the other children were jealous and angry. Catherine was unable to recall more of this episode, although she could remember that something else had happened.

The next encounter occurred when she was seven. She was walking down an alleyway when she saw "a little white thing", which turned out to be a man with a big bald head and big eyes. He told her he wanted to take her somewhere, and she objected because her parents had told her not to go with strange people. Nevertheless, he took her arm and they flew up through the air and in through a hole – presumably in a UFO – and into a room.

There, he told her that he was going to make a little cut in her finger because he needed a sample. She protested vociferously, in spite of which he made a little cut on the forefinger of her left hand, and took a blood sample. He explained that he was researching "your planet" "We're trying to stop the damage from pollution." Then Catherine found herself once again back in the alleyway, and when she rejoined some friends watching cartoons on television, no one had noticed that she had been absent for a quarter of an hour.

Finally, under hypnosis, she was able to recall what had happened when she lost the forty-five minutes in February 1991. She had driven into a wooded area, and stopped, after which she experienced a kind of paralysis. Something opened the driver's door, and guided her out of the car. She was taken up into a huge ship, where several aliens tried to remove her clothes. She got angry, and asked them why they didn't go and rent a porn movie. Then it dawned on her that they didn't know what a porn movie was, and did not understand the concept of voyeurism. After this, she was taken into an enormous room "the size of an airplane hanger", in which there were hundreds of tables, and hundreds of human beings lying on them. After the usual physical examination, during which a black-eyed alien soothed her and made her feel better, a metal tube was inserted in her vagina, and then another thinner instrument was used to reach up inside her. When it came out again, it seemed to be holding something like a foetus. Her guess was that it must be about three months old. The aliens seemed unable to understand her anger at being treated in this way, and she was finally "floated" back to her car.

It had been her impression that the foetus was about

three months old. When John Mack asked her about this, she recalled how, about three months before the episode, she had found herself driving in the middle of the night along deserted roads, and had pulled off the highway at a rest stop. She thinks she sat there for about fifteen minutes – with a sensation as if she was waiting for something – and when nothing happened, drove off home again. It now struck her as possible that this was the time when she was "impregnated".

As a result of her hypnotic sessions with John Mack, Catherine found that she was able to come to terms – to some extent – with what was happening to her. The sense of outrage began to give way to a feeling of curiosity about what the aliens wanted to achieve. She also noted that her intuitions had improved, and that she can feel "auras", and is more attuned to the emotional states of other people. "This whole experience makes you open up to so many levels, so many other possibilities. Everyone has these kinds of abilities, but we shut them off . . . ."

In July 1991, Catherine told John Mack that she believed something had happened two nights before. At a hypnotic session, she was finally able to describe this. A light, like a huge searchlight, streamed into her bedroom, and she passed through the window, the porch and a tree and saw her apartment building receding below her. She entered through a hole in the floor of the craft, and was taken into a kind of conference room, which she knew to be an illusion implanted in her mind. This was verified when the conference room melted away to reveal the actual room they were in. When she objected that they had concocted the conference room for her benefit, she was told, "We have to have a

143

UFO photographed by farmer Paul Trent, 1950.

conference, so you have to think its a conference, so we're taking you to a conference room so that you can be in that kind of serious frame of mind instead of making your usual smart-ass remarks that you always do." Catherine commented, "When this happened, I was just starting not to fight them. I was just at the very beginning. I'm not where I am now . . . ." After this, she was shown scenes of nature on a screen including the Grand Canyon. After this, there were pyramids, pictures of pharoahs and hieroglyphics. After this, they showed her a picture of a tomb painting, then she saw herself painting it. In this earlier incarnation she was a man, and she felt, "this makes sense to me . . . . this is not a trick." Mack questioned her at some length about her life as a painter, and was struck by the amount she seemed to know – for example about the process of mixing paint, about the man's clothing and head-dress. During this process, Catherine apparently became the painter, whom she called Akremenon. She was able to describe in detail precisely what she was painting, the different-sized figures on the panel (royalty had to be larger than commoners), and the problems of proportion involved. She said that the pharaoh for whom she was working had "demoted" various gods, and Mack speculates that it could have been the pharaoh Akhenaton.

Now, for the first time, Catherine began to feel that the aliens were offering her something that she could understand. When she asked them why they used such "theatrics" they explained, "To make you understand, to comprehend the implications. To put you in the right frame of mind." She came to feel that certain emotions like love, caring, helpfulness, compassion are "the key", whereas others like anger, hatred and fear are "not useful", especially fear. "Fear is like the worst one. They were trying to get me to get over fear, and that's why they were trying to scare me so badly, because I would eventually get sick of it, and get over it, and get on to the more important things." As a result of her new attitude, Catherine was able to play a more active part in the abductee support group conducted by Mack.

There is a sense in which Mack's attitude to the whole abduction phenomenon is more creative and positive than that of any other investigator. "A number of abductees with whom I have worked experience at certain points an opening up to the sort of being in the cosmos, which they often call Home, and from which they feel they have been brutally cut off in the course of becoming embodied as a human being. They may weep ecstatically when during our sessions they experience an opening or return to Home. They may . . . . rather resent having to remain on Earth in embodied form, even as they realise that on Earth they have some sort of mission to assist in bringing about a change in human consciousness."

In speaking of the philosophical implications of the abduction experience, Mack writes, "Quite a few abductees have spoken to me of their sense that at least some of their experiences are not occurring within the physical space/time dimensions of the universe as we comprehend it. They speak of aliens breaking through from another dimension, through a 'slit' or 'crack' in some sort of barrier, entering our world from 'beyond the veil.' Abductees, some of whom have little education to prepare them to explain about such abstractions or odd dislocations, will speak of the collapse of space/ time that occurs during their experiences. They experience the aliens, indeed their abductions themselves, as happening in another reality, although one that is as powerfully actual to them as – or more so than – the familiar physical world." One of his abductees said, "You can't really evaluate it in the language and physical descriptive terms of this dimension because it wasn't really happening here. It was half happening here and half happening somewhere else." Catherine had told him that she remembered some place between times of incarnation on Earth where bodies were not solid, appearing only in kind of energy outline. "This was before any of us had lives here. This place is in a totally different universe. It's not in our earth space/time dimension." Another abductee said: "All times can come to one place. This is real. It's not philosophical. I can really go to another time frame and [my experiences] can pull me from other time frames to here."

In a section entitled "Spiritual Implications", Mack compares the abductors to Zen Buddhist masters who use shock treatment as a teaching method. "The alien beings that abductees speak about seem to many of them to come from another domain that is felt to be closer to the source of being or primary creation. They have been described, however homely their appearance, as intermediaries or emissaries from God, even as angels . . . . the acknowledgement of their existence, after the initial ontological shock, is sometimes . . . . the first step in the opening of consciousness to a universe that is no longer simply material. Abductees come to appreciate that the universe is filled with intelligences and is itself intelligent. They develop a sense of awe before a mysterious cosmos that becomes sacred and ensouled. The sense of separation from all the rest of creation breaks down and the experience of oneness becomes an essential aspect of the evolution of the abductees' consciousness . . . ." He adds, "The aliens themselves may come to be seen as a split-off part of the abductees' soul or Self."

In a section called "FURTHER IMPLICATIONS FOR HUMAN CONSCIOUSNESS", Mack writes, "Abduction experiences also open the consciousness of abductees, as I work with them, to cycles of birth and death that are reminiscent of the Tibetan transitional realities or *Bardos*. This is most clearly illustrated in the past life experiences that are emerging increasingly in our sessions as I have become willing to listen to them. These reports suggest that individual consciousness may have its own line of development, separate from the body."

It is significant that Mack associates some of these implications with the ideas put forward by his friend Thomas Kuhn, the author of the influential *Structure of Scientific Revolutions*. Kuhn argues that scientists imagine that science is a "wide open" discipline, whose only purpose is to expand human knowledge, and whose approach is always free of prejudice. Kuhn suggests that, on the contrary, scientists are inclined to develop an unconscious attitude which is closer to that of orthodox churchmen, outraged by anyone who does not accept their basic dogmas. He goes on to suggest that what he calls "paradigm shifts" only come about as a result of violent upheavals, which sometimes involve individual scientists being treated as pariahs and outcasts. Mack argues that "the experiences recounted by the abductees with whom I have worked during the past four years constitute, I think, a rich body of evidence to support the idea that the cosmos, far from being devoid of meaning and intelligence, is . . . . 'informed by some kind of universal intelligence', an intelligence 'of scarcely conceivable power, complexity and aesthetic subtlety yet one to which the human intelligence is akin, and in which it can participate.' "

John Mack's view is supported by the widely publicised books of another abductee, Whitley Strieber. In *Communion, a True Story* (1987), Strieber describes his own experiences of abduction, beginning – apparently – on December 26, 1985, in his secluded log cabin in up-state New York. He woke up in the middle of the night with a sense that something was wrong, and saw an "alien visitor" coming in through the door. It was about three foot six inches tall, had the usual oval shaped head, and enormous black eyes set at a slant. After this, he was taken out of the house, and into some kind of spacecraft. His impression was that the alien who seemed to be in charge was female. He was shown a box containing a kind of thin hypodermic needle, and told that this was going to be inserted into his brain. His reaction was to scream, and when the woman asked him, "What can we do to make you stop screaming?", his reply was. "You could let me smell you." (He admits that many of his reactions and responses seem, in retrospect, to be completely illogical, like those in a dream.)

He was undressed, and laid down on a table with his legs apart, after which some kind of device was inserted into his rectum. After this, they made an incision in his forefinger. Suddenly he found himself back in his bed, with no memory whatsoever of what had happened. It seemed to him that a barn owl had looked in through his window, but when he looked at the roof, he saw there were no tracks in the snow. For some time before this, Strieber and his wife had been experiencing a great deal of conflict, due to – as he acknowledges – "my demands and accusatory behaviour." "At the time I had no idea that I was suffering from emotional trauma, or that dozens of other people had been through very similar ordeals after being taken by the visitors." He found that his ability to concentrate suddenly vanished. He experienced a sudden pain behind his right ear, and his wife noticed a tiny pinpoint of a scab. Reading a book called *Science and the UFOs* he suddenly found that he was unable to go on reading, and had to slam it shut. His suspicion that he had been abducted finally led him to contact Budd Hopkins, who, it turned out, lived only a few blocks away from him in New York.

From this point on, Strieber's account echoes that of many other abductees. Hypnosis by Dr Donald Klein, who had had no experience of abductees, and therefore could not ask leading questions, gradually began to uncover a whole series of abduction experiences that had been taking place since his childhood. There were whole days – in one case weeks – of "missing time". He became increasingly certain that his wife and son had also been abducted or had some contact with the aliens. Participation in an "abduction support group" made him aware that there were dozens – probably thousands – of people like himself. And, like John Mack's Catherine, he gradually came to feel that these unpleasant experiences could be used positively, in the cause of personal evolution.

7

Final Proof or Total Fantasy? – Moon Monuments, Martian Cities and the Cydonian Sphinx

Some researchers claim that NASA has found, and concealed, undeniable evidence of alien life on our two nearest solar neighbors – Mars and the Moon. If so, why cover up the most astounding (and budget-expanding) discovery of all time? This chapter looks at the arguments that may settle the issue of alien existence once and for all.

Life on Mars?

Evidence of intelligent life on Mars was first discovered in 1877. In that year the Italian astronomer Giovanni Schiaparelli announced that, using a state-of-the-art telescope, he had distinguished "canals" criss-crossing the surface of the red planet. Up to that time, astronomers had only been able to pick out dark and light areas on Mars' surface – much as our Moon appears to the naked eye. These were speculatively described by some observers as seas and desert landscapes. Schiaparelli's discovery sent conjecture running wild – planet-spanning canals suggested that intelligent, organised, even civilised life might exist on Mars. Schiaparelli himself was reported to be unhappy with the furore caused by his announcement. In his report he had used the word "canali" – to describe the net-like markings. In Italian, the word means both canal (a man-made waterway) and channel (a natural watercourse), the latter being his intended meaning. As a scientist he disliked conclusions based on insufficient data. Nevertheless, by the same standard, he did not discount the possibility that the remarkably straight "canali" might be artificial structures.

Schiaparelli was not the first to observe possible signs of non-terrestrial civilisation; fifty-three years earlier, a German physician and astronomer, Baron Franz von Paula Gruithuisen, claimed to have found "many distinct traces (that proved the existence) of lunar inhabitants", including a "city" just north of the Schroter Crater, delineated by a series of curiously symmetrical hills or mounds. In the latter years of the nineteenth century, other astronomers claimed to be able to see the Martian lines, and some even produced maps of the Mars network. As telescopes increased in power, astronomers reported shaded areas bordering the canals that might suggest the existence of vegetation. Clouds in the atmosphere and polar icecaps were also recorded, indicating climatic similarities to Earth. Mathematicians calculated that the canals must be over 70 miles wide, suggesting a monumental construction programme by the Martians. (It is interesting to note that the Victorians generally took it for granted, that the Martians were as human – "fashioned in the likeness of God" – as themselves.)

Skeptics pointed out that Mars, with a much lower mass than that of the Earth, would be bound to have a lower gravity and a thinner atmosphere. This, in turn, would increase the evaporation rate and greatly restrict the amount of surface water available to the Martians. To counter such criticism, Percival Lowell, one of the pioneers of modern astronomy and a keen advocate of Martian civilisation, suggested that Mars was an ancient, dying world, desperately controlling its precious liquid resources through canals. The idea caught the popular imagination, so when Nicola Tesla and Marconi – rivals for the title of the inventor of the radio – separately announced that they had received signals from the red planet, many people wondered if the Martians were appealing for help. Others, like the science fiction writer H. G. Wells, warned that they might be preparing for a war to seize our planet.

The best method to communicate with creatures from other worlds has long been a bone of contention among scientists. On January 3, 1893, for example, the respected astronomer Sir Robert Ball addressed the Royal Academy of Science in London, on the impossibility of communication with Mars: "The necessary flag," he explained, "would have to be as big as Ireland. How such a flag could be waved in a manner to attract the people of Mars I dare not suggest."

Seven years later, in 1900, the American scientist R. A. Fessenden demonstrated a simpler method of sending long-distance messages, by transmitting his voice via radio waves.

Perhaps it is fortunate then that the giant reflector telescopes of the late twentieth century have burst that speculative bubble. We now know that the "canals" are an optical illusion caused by the eye's tendency to link up small, blurred, dot-like features, and that the dark patches on Mars are not seas, just darker areas of desert. The "Mariner 4" probe in 1965 revealed that the planet has only 1% the atmosphere of Earth and is extremely cold. Later "Mariner" probes also discovered that the Martian icecaps are made predominantly of carbon dioxide, not water. Since, under the circumstances it seems doubtful that Mars could support life, most scientist have naturally ceased to search for evidence of Martians. Scrutiny of our other neighboring worlds, the Moon and Venus, has also caused us to abandon the search for Selenites (Moon-men) and Venusians. (Our Moon is a barren ball of rock, too small to retain an atmosphere, while the atmosphere of Venus consists of corrosive acid vapor with a surface temperature of 900 degrees.) In spite of which, most people agree that it is unlikely that the Earth is the only planet in the universe that supports life.

Accounts of the US-Soviet space race have tended to emphasise the cold war, and the political aspects of the space programmes – from Sputnik to Star Wars. Yet, another fundamental motive has been the hope of discovering evidence for extraterrestrial life. Although NASA (the National Aeronautical and Space Administration) was set up in America in 1958 in direct response to the Soviet launch of "Sputnik" in 1957, Congress specified the search for alien life as one of its basic objectives.

Moon Monuments

So far, probes to the Moon, Venus, Mars and other planets have failed to find any evidence of life. In spite of which, there is a widespread belief among monitoring groups – particularly those interested in UFOs – that

NASA, the other government agencies and even the former Soviet space bureau have been concealing evidence that other planets in our solar system have been, and may continue to be, inhabited. The proof, claim these "conspiracy theorists" can be found in the space agencies' own files.

This was the argument of a group calling themselves "The Enterprise Mission" – made up of scientists, engineers and other space-related researchers (some of whom were former NASA employees) – who called a press conference in at the National Press Club in Washington DC on March 21, 1996. Their spokesman, science journalist and ex-NASA advisor Richard Hoagland, portentously described the purpose of the meeting as "the announcement of the millennium". What followed was the presentation of what Hoagland claimed to be "thirty-year-old suppressed evidence revealing ancient artificial structures on the Moon", including "photos [that] show astronauts walking amid apparent Lunar ruins, on 'leaked' NASA and Soviet space photographs." The meeting was well attended by members of the world press, but produced less of a sensation than the group was hoping for. Journalists found the speeches boring and the photographic "evidence" blurry and unconvincing. The *Washington Post* subsequently printed a scathing article headlined "GREEN CHEESE AND BALONEY", which accurately represented the general reaction of the media. Hoagland's call for the White House to publish the NASA files on "alien artefacts" went unanswered.

With hindsight the failure of Hoagland's "Enterprise Mission" to gain media support seems totally predictable. Their "evidence" looked and sounded too absurd to be true. Skepticism is the natural mind-set of the journalist. He is interested in fact, and is only willing to swallow speculation provided it is mixed with a healthy roughage of fact. "Computer-enhanced" photographs are bound to arouse mistrust and incredulity, since no one can be sure how far "enhancement" is merely a reflection of wishful thinking.

In issue 90 of the *Fortean Times*, editor Bob Rickard lists some of the photographs presented by Hoagland. These included; "The Shard" – a 1.5 mile-tall, possibly helical, spire of meteorite-damaged glass, "the Castle", described as "a geometric, glittering glass object hanging more than nine miles above the surface of the Moon", "the Cube" – a complex "megacube" on top of a seven mile-high tower, "the Spire" – a 20 mile-high, undamaged version of the Shard, in the Mare Crisium, and "The City" a Los Angeles-sized city-block grid pattern in the northeast Ukert region, near an unusual, square-shaped crater. These and a number of ruined "glass-like, highly complex domes" were all detected on photographs taken by Apollo astronauts and by NASA and Soviet satellites, which have been released over the last thirty years. One is even described as showing "Apollo 12" astronaut Alan Bean standing amid "tiers of glass-like ruins", presumably to lend scale to the picture. And why, if their intention was a cover-up, should NASA (and/or its Russian equivalent) allow the photographs to become generally available? Hoagland suggested that perhaps no one at NASA had actually noticed the controversial shots – image processing had undergone a revolution since they were taken, and some of the "discoveries" were made only through using most modern computer techniques. His alternative suggestion was that NASA had simply expected them to pass unnoticed among so many millions of other pictures.

Predictably, NASA flatly denied the existence of artificial structures on the Moon, and most of the press were inclined to take their word – many citing the imaginary "canals" that had so convinced Lowell and his contemporaries. Yet evidence for Hoagland's arguments have continued to accumulate as astronomers have observed formations on the Moon that seem to defy normal explanation. Among these are the "Blair Cuspids" (seven 600-foot-tall obelisks on the Sea of Tranquillity), the "Straight Wall" (a 70-mile-long, 1200-foot-tall structure also known as the "Railway", due to its remarkable straightness) and the "Bridge over the Sea of Crisis" (a 12-mile-long structure whose formation and continued survival baffles astronomers and geologists alike.)

NASA has also inadvertently added to the mystification; some of their lunar discoveries, published following the various "Apollo" missions, are certainly bizarre. For instance, the rocks brought back from the Moon have been dated between 3.6 and 5.3 billion years old – which raises problems, since the Earth itself is only 3.7 billion years old. Moreover, moon soil samples have proved to be about a billion years older than the rocks, leading some scientists to theorize that the Moon is older than our Sun and therefore must have originated outside the solar system. Odder still, the Moon appears to be hollow (just as H. G. Wells suggested in *The First Men on the Moon*.) That at least was the only explanation offered when astronauts reported that impacting objects – like meteorites and spent rocket sections – caused the ground to "ring like a gong or a bell". Some of the more exuberant extraterrestrial archaeologists have even suggested that the Moon might be an (abandoned?) interstellar spaceship.

Sherlock Holmes had more than one occasion to warn Watson that it is a mistake to jump to conclusions without knowing the full facts. He would certainly have repeated the same advice to both the extraterrestrial archaeologists and the space agencies – the former for jumping to premature conclusions, the latter for stating so dogmatically that these conclusions are nonsense. Yet it must be added that it is hard to see what else can be done, since the physical evidence is so far away from Earth, and space exploration funding is at an all time low. Of course, for the non-expert, it would clarify matters somewhat if the extraterrestrial archaeologists and NASA could agree on any of the data we *do* have to hand. Fortunately, on one striking discovery, they do . . . . almost.

In July 1976, during the US Bicentennial celebrations, NASA placed an unmanned spacecraft in orbit around Mars. The "Viking 1" probe would, it was hoped, finally obtain the positive, unarguable facts about Mars, first from a robotic "lander" and second from detailed orbital photographs. (Previous probes had managed only quick "sling-shot" swoops around the planet.) The lander dashed any remaining hopes that Mars might sustain life – its instruments confirmed the minimal atmosphere, the appalling cold and the waterless, sterile soil.

At the same time the Viking Orbiter, freed of its robotic load, carried on circling the planet at a thousand miles above the surface. It photographed many amazing natural features, such as the Olympus Mons, a fifteen-mile high extinct volcano covering the area of a medium-sized country. But those who hoped for life on Mars – which meant everybody – were unconsoled by such astonishing features; they wanted aliens, not geology lessons. (Significantly, funding for space programs plummeted dramatically after the "Viking" project. If NASA had been less positive about its findings – which after all, covered only a small area of the planet's surface – the taxpayer would have continued to generously fund the search for aliens and the space agency might have built a Moonbase by now.)

Cydonian Sphinx

"Viking 1" had been sending back pictures of Mars for several weeks when a NASA researcher called Toby Owen made an interesting discovery. Poring over the pictures of an area called the Plain of Cydonia, he found what looked like a pair of eyes looking back at him. In the upper third of frame 35A72 was a human face – a mile-long, rectangular mesa (or contoured plateau) with two eyes, a nose and a suggestion of a mouth. At that time, NASA was still holding regular press conferences. Owen's supervisors, perhaps hoping to arouse some enthusiasm in the increasingly jaded press corps, presented the "Face" picture at the following meeting as a mild joke. The NASA spokesman smiled as he said, "Isn't it peculiar what tricks of lighting and shadow can do?"

NASA realised too late what story-hungry pressmen can do. They seemed to regard it as the most exciting evidence since Percival Lowell's canals, and the headlines reflected this. Suddenly, Martians were once again on the agenda. NASA hastily tried to back-pedal, repeating with increasing emphasis that the face was merely a trick of light. The Cydonian mesa looked unnaturally symmetrical in the photograph, they explained, because of the angle of the light. The setting sun was low to the horizon when the picture was taken, causing a large part of one side of the feature – the right cheek and jaw – to be covered with deep shadow. A second picture, they said, taken a few hours later, revealed the mesa to be merely an unsymmetrical mass of rock. The pressmen asked to see the picture and, after an uncomfortable pause, the official replied that it was not presently available. Oddly enough, this seemed to satisfy the reporters – who had no reason to doubt the official spokesman – and the matter was soon forgotten. It now seems unlikely that NASA actually knew of a second "Face" picture at that time. The spokesman mentioned that it had been taken "a few hours later," but since the sun was setting in the first picture, a "few hours" would carry Cydonia into the night zone, where no photographs could be taken. In fact, another photograph of the Face did exist, but it was not to be discovered for two and a half years.

In 1979, independent researchers Vincent DiPietro, an electrical engineer, and Gregory Molenaar, a computer scientist, became interested in the long-forgotten Face on Cydonia and set out to find the unpublished second photograph. The picture was not where NASA had said it should be, and the pair were forced to sort through thousands of photographs, but they did eventually find it. The new picture was taken not a few hours, but thirty-five days after the first one, and with the sunlight at a different angle. By cross-indexing the two images the researchers made a startling discovery. NASA was wrong: the mesa *was* symmetrical and did seem to have two eyes, a nose and a curving, ape-like mouth. Computer enhancement further suggested an "eyeball" in at least one of the sockets, "teeth" in the mouth and a hairline or cowl across the forehead.

The implications were, of course, stunning. Either the Face was the most bizarre accident of nature known to man, or it had been built by intelligent beings for an unknown purpose. To check the first possibility, DiPietro and Molenaar studied photographs of the surrounding Cydonian Plain, where similar natural conditions could reasonably be expected. Although they found several other strange formations, none seemed the result of the odd "erosion" that the face displayed. They considered the known effects of weathering, tectonic movement and even the impacts of meteorites, but none seemed to offer an explanation. Ten miles south-south-west of the Face mesa, DiPietro and Molenaar noted another oddly regular mountain. It was, in fact, shaped like a five-sided pyramid, having five triangular "sides" formed by five ridges that ran straight from the base to the pointed tip. The result looked more like a demonstration model in a geometry class than a natural formation. At the base of each ridge was a V formation that looked like a pile of sand or – as DiPietro and Molenaar commented – a supporting buttress. This, again, was not like natural weathering – the most eroded areas should be in the middle of the ridges, not at the bottom.

Cartographer Erol Torun made an examination of this pentagonal mountain – unofficially named the D&M Pyramid after its discoverers – and came up with some interesting results. Torun had previously worked for the US military's Defence Mapping Agency and was trained in the analysis of satellite photographs. In matters of national defence, it is sometimes vital to be able to tell the difference between natural and artificial structures – between normal hills and disguised missile silos, for example. (The astronomer Carl Sagan conducted a study of several hundred thousand satellite photographs in the 1960s and found only one which conclusively indicated the existence of intelligent life on Earth – admittedly, 1960's satellite technology was primitive even by 1976 Viking standards.) Although Torun could not say that the mountain was definitely artificial he stated that, despite his wide knowledge of geomorphology, he could think of "no known natural mechanism to account for the D&M Pyramid's formation . . . ." Moreover, when Torun came to examine the angles of the sides of the pyramid, he was amazed to discover that they exemplified many basic principles of geometry. So impressed was he by the unlikelihood of such precise geometrical relationships occurring accidentally, that he described the D&M Pyramid as the "Cydonian Rosetta Stone". [The Rosetta Stone was the parallel text in Greek and hieroglyphics that led to the decipherment of hieroglyphics.] Torun was implying not only that the pyramid was intelligently constructed, but that it contains a message for the mathematically literate.

When Richard Hoagland – later the spokesman for the "Enterprise Mission" – read DiPietro and Molenaar's findings on the Cydonian "artefacts", he found himself pondering on the practical question: where did the builders – if indeed there were builders – live? If we consider similar great monuments on Earth – the Sphinx or the Eiffel Tower, for example – they are always built in, or within sight of, cities. Looking for signs of habitation, Hoagland noted a dozen or so mounds about ten miles west-southwest of the Face. These, like the Face and the D&M Pyramid, did not seem to be obviously natural formations, having straight ridges and roughly geometric shapes. Furthermore, they seem to be distributed around a central "square", in the middle of which are four smaller mounds in a diamond pattern. Hoagland pointed out that anyone standing in the center of the "City Square" would have an excellent view of the Face in exact profile. (He also noted – as had DiPietro and Molenaar – that one of the ridges of the D&M Pyramid points directly at the Face.) It was Hoagland who coined the term "Martian Sphinx" to describe the Face, suggesting that it may have had a similar religious significance for its builders.

When "Apollo 11" landed on the Moon on July 21, 1969, the crew looked out on a wasteland devoid of life. That, at least, is what NASA has told the public, but others believe an alien welcoming committee was there to witness Neil Armstrong's first "small step."

The evidence comes from Dr Vladimir Azhazha, a Russian physicist and Professor of Mathematics at Moscow University. Dr Azhazha claims that the Soviets monitored all the transmissions between NASA and "Apollo 11". Shortly after the landing, the Russians eavesdropped as "Neil Armstrong relayed the message to Mission Control that two, large, mysterious objects were watching them." Obviously, he says, NASA removed this part of the transmission from the publicly broadcast material.

Maurice Chatelain, a communications specialist who was working for NASA in 1969, supports Dr Azhazha's claim. He has stated publicly that it was "common knowledge in NASA" that UFO's were buzzing around "Apollo 11" and that, indeed, all the Apollo missions were monitored by flying saucers.

The "Faceists" – a term coined by the media to describe students of the Cydonian anomalies – stress that although the "Viking" photographs are far from perfect, they appear to show constructed objects, not natural objects endowed with symmetry by some trick of the light. NASA agreed on the symmetry, but diverged sharply from the extraterrestrial archaeologists on the matter of interpretation. The view of the agency is that the formations must be natural, because Mars is too hostile to support life, even in its most basic forms.

Throughout the 1980s and early 1990s this view was widely accepted – but in 1996 it was suddenly challenged. In August of that year, a group of researchers working for the Johnson Space Center (a sub-branch of NASA) announced that they had found possible evidence of primitive life on Mars. They had cut open a meteorite labelled ALH84001 – recovered in 1984 in Antarctica – and found tiny tube-like structures that appear to be microfossils. The rock was dated 4.5 billion years ago, and the "microfossils" to about 3.6 billion years. Since there was little doubt that the meteorite had originated on Mars, hurled into space by some massive explosion or asteroid collision 15 million years ago, the team cautiously suggested that Mars may once have supported pre-amoebic life forms. Some Mars researchers disagreed, suggesting that the compounds could have been formed by non-living processes or that they may have infiltrated into the meteorite after it arrived on Earth. Yet, many other researchers accepted the possibility of life on Mars – for a quiet revolution has been taking place in Mars research, one which began even before the start of the "Viking" project in the 1970s, and was based on geological considerations.

From the time of the "Mariner 4" probe, in 1965, scientists accepted that Mars was as uninhabitable as the Moon. This was because the probe had revealed a great number of uneroded meteorite craters on the planet's surface. Millions of meteorites also strike the Earth, but its water-rich atmosphere soon erodes them. Since Mars had craters, the argument went, there could be no water in its atmosphere. This theory was itself eroded by subsequent Mars probes. The minimal summer melting of the Martian poles suggests that there is a large quantity of water ice beneath the frozen carbon dioxide. Better photographs of the surface showed fluid-worn ravines, dried lakes and even the beds of vanished seas scattered across the planet. Craters once thought unchanged since they were made have, in fact, revealed signs of apparent rain erosion. Such evidence made a powerful impact on Martian research. Many experts now believe that Mars, due to its widely varied angle of rotation, has enjoyed "hot" periods lasting sometimes over a million years. At these times, when the planet is warmer than zero centigrade, sub-surface water would be released to gush across the land and an atmosphere and rain would eventually be generated. It may be true that the Mars of today is as dead as the "Viking Lander" data suggested, but it may once have been no more bleak than the steppes of Central Asia.

Nevertheless, even million-year long "interglacials" would not be time enough for life to evolve to the monument and city building stage. If intelligent hands (or tentacles) built the Face, it is unlikely to have been the work of native Martians. The alternative is creatures alien to Mars, perhaps even leaving a message for mankind to decipher when it reached the stage of space exploration.

If this scenario sounds familiar, it is because the theme was explored in the science-fiction movie *2001*. Critics of the "Faceists" suggest they are distorting the facts (a few black and white satellite photographs) to buttress just such a fantasy. "Faceists", including the "Enterprise Mission", retort that NASA must know perfectly well that Cydonia was once inhabited, but has hushed up the evidence. The reason behind this suspicion comes from a report made by the influential Brookings Institute during the creation of NASA in 1958. This study, which is said to have been central to the space agency's development, pointed out that whenever two different cultures collide for the first time the result for both is always shattering and, occasionally, terminal for one or the other. (For example, the Europeans and the Native Americans, the Mongols and the Europeans, the Americans and the Vietnamese. . . .) The effect on religions that claim man as some kind of exclusive creation of God would be traumatic, and as to the political repercussions, the Brookings Institute could not even speculate about the full extent of the shock to the system.

The report concluded that evidence of intelligent alien life should only released to the public with the greatest caution. It was this advice, the "Faceists" suggest, that led to the great Cydonia cover-up. New NASA probes, due to orbit and photograph Mars in late 1997 and 1998, will provide much improved pictures of the Plain of Cydonia. But unless these photographs reveal far more detail, it seems likely that the debate on alien artefacts will continue until geologists and archaeologists can examine the evidence at first hand.

Index